HINDU BELIEFS AND ISSUES

Michael Keene

Badger Publishing Limited
15 Wedgwood Gate
Pin Green Industrial Estate
Stevenage, Hertfordshire SG1 4SU
Telephone: 01438 356907
Fax: 01438 747015
www.badger-publishing.co.uk
enquiries@badger-publishing.co.uk

Badger KS3 Religious Education
Hindu Beliefs and Issues

First published 2007
ISBN 978-1-84691-087-6

Acknowledgements
Photos © Alex Keene, The Walking Camera, with the following exceptions:
3 Gandhi © Popperfoto; 10 Yoga © Around the world in a viewfinder;
11, 31 Beggar © Stuart Dunn Travel; 13 Naming © World Religions Photo Library;
19 Child © Dinodia Images; 20 Elderly © Keren Su/China Span; 22 Playground © Alan Weildon; 26 Nandi © Robert Harding Picture Library; 29 Krishna © ArkReligion.com;
33 Dalit © Butch Martin / **Alamy**.
12 Couple, 16 Wedding, 30 Sari © Vijay Pathak.
15 Sacred thread © World Illustrated/Photoshot.
21 Wealth © Sipa Press / Poverty © Patrick Lucero; 22 Hospital © Sipa Press; 25 Tree © Image Source / **Rex Features**.
23 © Bhaktivedanta Manor Archives, reproduced with kind permission.

Publisher: David Jamieson
Editor: Paul Martin
Designer: Adam Wilmott
Cover photo: Alex Keene, The Walking Camera
Illustrator: Juliet Breese

Printed in Great Britain by Ashford Colour Press Ltd, Gosport, Hampshire

CONTENTS

WHAT IS HINDUISM?

It is not easy to pinpoint exactly how, when or where the religion of Hinduism began. Unlike the other major world religions, the teachings of Hinduism cannot be traced back to a single teacher or founder, such as **Jesus** in Christianity or **Muhammad** in Islam. Instead, the teachings of Hinduism come from many different ancient religious thinkers who lived at different times in history. Their teachings have been gathered together in many holy books.

THE ORIGINS OF HINDUISM

The roots of Hinduism are found in the Indus Valley civilisation which grew up around the banks of the River Indus in India in about 2000 BCE. This civilisation was very advanced, with people living in large houses and towns and producing a highly glazed form of pottery.

The prosperity of this group, however, began to decline in around 500 BCE as a group of people called the Aryans moved into India. They built great cities along the River Ganges and intermarried with the Indus people. Their religions also intermingled and it was out of this mixture that Hinduism grew. The Aryans provided Hindus with some of their most important holy books [unit 18].

An avatar is when God visits the Earth in human form. Krishna, an avatar of the god **Vishnu**, is the most popular of all Hindu avatars.

UNDERSTANDING HINDUISM

1 The ultimate aim of every Hindu is to reach **moksha** [liberation] through becoming united with God [**Brahman**]. To reach this stage, each person must pass through a cycle of many births and deaths [unit 10]. The words in extract A, from the **Bhagavad-Gita**, are recited at every Hindu cremation.

A   *"Worn-out garments are shed by the body;*
Worn-out bodies are shed by the dweller;
Within the body new bodies are donned
by the dweller like garments."

Bhagavad-Gita 2.22

2 To control the way that a person lives, Hinduism provides certain 'disciplines'. A life-span is divided into four **ashramas** or stages [unit 4]:

- the time of training or education
- the time of the householder
- the time of retirement
- the time of the holy man

TAKE TIME TO THINK

The ultimate aim of every Hindu is to obtain spiritual liberation. What would you say is your ultimate aim in life?

3 To reach moksha, a person must live a righteous life, work hard, prosper and enjoy the good things in life. All of these should be reached by the end of the second ashrama. Time can then be set aside especially to reach moksha.

4 Each person has 'a spark of God' in them but it shines more brightly in some than others. Those who possess the brightest spark are the **avatars**. The avatars are sent by Brahman to restore righteousness on Earth:

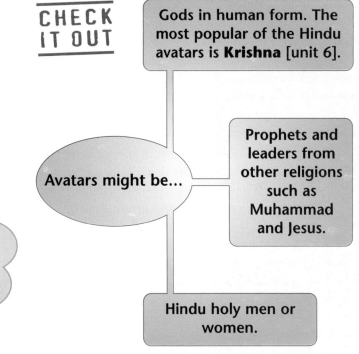

CHECK IT OUT

Gods in human form. The most popular of the Hindu avatars is **Krishna** [unit 6].

Avatars might be...

Prophets and leaders from other religions such as Muhammad and Jesus.

Hindu holy men or women.

OVER TO YOU ▶▶▶

1 Imagine that you are trying to explain to a friend one way in which Hinduism is different to the other major world religions. What would you say to them?

2 How do scholars think that the religion of Hinduism began?

3 You are introduced here to some very important Hindus words. Explain in a single sentence or two the meaning of:
   a) Brahman
   b) Moksha
   c) Ashrama
   d) Avatar
   e) Krishna

THE CASTE SYSTEM

In traditional Indian society, the **Brahmins**, or priests, are at the top of the Caste System.

To understand the **Caste System** in India, it is very important that you understand three ideas:

THE JATI

Hindus everywhere attach great importance to the group in society, called the **jati**, into which they have been born. Originally, each jati was linked to an occupation and members of the jati all followed the same occupation. They would belong, for example, to the 'shoemakers' jati' or the 'leather workers' jati'.

Nowadays, people have more educational opportunities than in the past and it is common to move to find work. Now members of a jati can get jobs which are quite different to the traditional occupation of members of their group. This is especially true for Indians living in Western countries and in the larger cities of India.

In the villages of India, however, there has been far less change. A person's jati can still affect where they are able to live, who they can marry and who they can mix with. It is still usual for Hindus – even those living in a Western country – to marry someone from their own group or jati.

OVER TO **YOU** ▶▶▶

1 When a Hindu says that they belong to a 'jati', what are they talking about?

2 Why are the 'jatis' of most Hindus less important now than they used to be?

3 Describe the four varnas.

TAKE TIME TO THINK

Why do you think that modern Hindus in India are finding it very difficult to do away with varnas altogether?

VARNAS

The dividing of Indian society into groups goes back to ancient times. The **Rig-Veda**, the very important and earliest of the Hindu holy books, describes four **varnas** or 'colours':

1   The **Brahmins** [priests]. These are men in the community who are given the responsibility of keeping alive the traditions and teachings of Hinduism. They are expected to understand, and pass on, the religious teachings of Hinduism. They must set a good example to others by remaining pure in word and deed.

2   The **Kshatriyas**. These are people given the responsibility of leading and ruling others. They must make the decisions in their community and protect the poor and weak. In the past, they have been the rulers and the fighters.

3   The **Vaishyas**. The goods for sale and the wealth in society come from members of this group. They are the business people and the shop-owners.

4   The **Shudras**. These people are those who carry out the manual and physical work which every community needs. They serve the needs of the other castes. They are craft-workers and servants.

There is another group of people who do not belong to any caste. Until about 50 years ago, they were called the **Untouchables**, but they are now called the **Dalits**. They are not even a varna and they are treated very badly.

> *We belong to the 'mochi' [shoemakers]. My grandfather was a shoemaker in Mumbai, or Bombay as it was then, but he felt that education was very important. My father is now a doctor in London. We meet with other members of our jati in Brixham, in a hall that we have paid for, and built, ourselves. I feel that I have a very close bond with them.*
>
> Hassan, 16

THE CASTE SYSTEM

Later, varnas became incorrectly mixed with castes and this caused problems. Castes or 'jatis' were smaller groups, often linked to occupations. In modern India, the traditions of caste are less strictly observed, but they still exist and they still affect the lives of millions of people, especially those from the lower varnas, today.

This is the traditional Caste System which has operated in India for centuries.

MAHATMA GANDHI

The man who came to be called Mahatma ['Great Soul'] **Gandhi** was born Mohandas Gandhi on 2nd October 1869. He became an outstanding figure in modern India and a famous religious personality who was much loved throughout the world.

THE EARLY GANDHI

In 1888, Gandhi studied law in England before becoming a lawyer in South Africa. He spoke out for the rights of Indians living there. Even at an early age, he was prepared to break the law for his beliefs but never to use violence.

Gandhi returned to India in 1915, where he set up a religious community based on his beliefs. In this community, life was very simple, with everyone being equal. These words were always included in the morning prayer service:

A *"We will be non-violent; we will be truthful; we will not steal; we will not keep more than we need. We will work with our hands; we will eat simple foods. We will work to set the Untouchables free."*

Gandhi was strongly opposed to the Caste System [unit 2]. He wanted the Untouchables, those outside the Caste System, to be able to go into the Hindu temples and mix freely with other Hindus. He took an Untouchable family into his community and renamed them **Harijans** – children of God.

GANDHI'S FAST

In 1932, Gandhi began a fast to protest against the treatment of the Untouchables. He said:

B *"I believe that, if untouchability is rooted out, it will cleanse Hinduism of a terrible crime... My cry will rise to the throne of Almighty God."*

As a result of the fast, many things improved for the Untouchables:

CHECK IT OUT

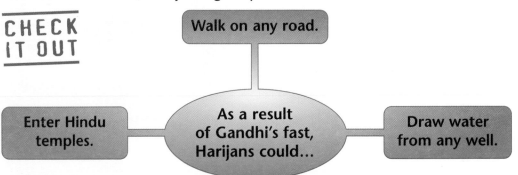

Walk on any road.

Enter Hindu temples.

As a result of Gandhi's fast, Harijans could...

Draw water from any well.

Much, though, remained the same. The life of Untouchables, or Dalits, is still very difficult.

He also led marches, such as the Salt March in 1930. The British rulers in India put a tax on salt and Gandhi led marchers on a 'sit in'. The marchers were beaten but they didn't respond violently. This led to some more changes in India.

Mahatma Gandhi leading a peaceful march. The authorities did not know how to deal with it.

THE DEATH OF GANDHI

At midnight on 14 August 1947, India won its fight for freedom from Britain. It had done so by using Gandhi's two main weapons – truth and non-violence. Less than six months later, Gandhi was dead. He was shot by an assassin as he stood for prayers. The Prime Minister of India said, on hearing of his death:

C *"The light that shone in this country was no ordinary light. It will illumine this country for many more years and, a thousand years later, it will still be seen in this country."*

TAKE TIME TO THINK

Think of one conflict that you have heard and read about recently. Do you think that it would have been better if another solution had been found to the problem?

OVER TO **YOU ▶▶▶**

1 If someone wants to fight with you, there are three things you can do:
   • Walk away.
   • Fight them.
   • Stand up to them but refuse to fight.
   Which of the three would you choose to do? Explain why.

2 When someone well-known dies, a tribute, called an obituary, is paid to them in the newspaper. It describes the good and interesting things that the person has done. Write an obituary for Gandhi that might have appeared in a newspaper in 1947.

THE FOUR ASHRAMAS

For male Hindus in the top three castes, people who are called 'the twice-born', the journey through life is made up of four ashramas or stages. From birth to death, a Hindu is concerned to answer the basic questions of life:

- Why am I here?
- What is life all about?
- What happens to me after I die?

While no-one can hope to find more than a small fraction of the answers to life's great questions, it is the search that is all important.

STAGE 1 – THE STUDENT

This stage begins when the **sacred thread** is placed around the neck of a boy and he is born-again [unit 15]. At the end of this ceremony, the boy is placed under the guidance of a **guru** or spiritual teacher. In the past, children left home to study with the guru but now they just visit him from time to time. Without the help of a guru, however, no-one can make real progress in their spiritual search.

STAGE 2 – THE HOUSEHOLDER

The student stage – covering a child's education – ends when a Hindu man decides to marry and take on family responsibilities. Through bringing children into the world, a Hindu is given the opportunity to achieve three goals:

1. A release from all basic human desires and energies through marriage, having children and bringing them up.

2. To contribute to the well-being of society through hard work.

3. To carry out the duties that their caste places on a person.

STAGE 3 – RETIREMENT

When a Hindu retires from active work, the circle returns to the beginning. He is now expected to become a student again as he studies the holy texts and talks to the gurus. Now he sets out to find answers to the two most difficult questions of all:

- What is the universe, and life itself, really all about?

- How do I discover my true self?

A few Hindus leave work early to seek the answers. When his first grandchild is born, a Hindu can, by tradition, leave his family and devote himself to prayer, study and **meditation**. As extract A shows, the forest is the traditional place to which a man retires:

A **"***When the householder sees his skin wrinkled and his hair white and the sons of his sons. Then he should retire to the forest.***"**

The Laws of Manu

This Hindu holy man is searching for the meaning of life and trying to find his true self.

STAGE 4 – THE SPIRITUAL PILGRIM

Only those men who have left their family and possessions behind can enter into this fourth stage.

CHECK IT OUT

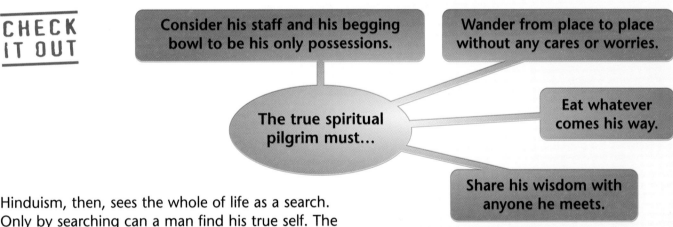

The true spiritual pilgrim must...

Consider his staff and his begging bowl to be his only possessions.

Wander from place to place without any cares or worries.

Eat whatever comes his way.

Share his wisdom with anyone he meets.

Hinduism, then, sees the whole of life as a search. Only by searching can a man find his true self. The start of the search is the beginning of life itself. The end is moksha.

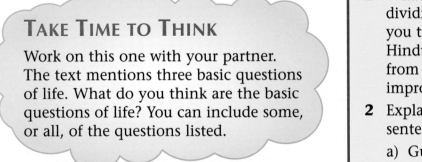

TAKE TIME TO THINK

Work on this one with your partner. The text mentions three basic questions of life. What do you think are the basic questions of life? You can include some, or all, of the questions listed.

OVER TO **YOU** ▶▶▶

1 What do you think about the idea of dividing life up into four stages? Do you think the four stages of Hinduism accurately reflect your life from beginning to end or can you improve on it?

2 Explain, in no more than two sentences, the meaning of:
   a) Guru
   b) Ashrama

ONE GOD IN MANY FORMS

You will find out

- About Brahman.
- The Hindu Trimurti.

In the glossary

Atman

Avatar

Brahma

Brahman

Krishna

Pantheism

Reincarnation

Shiva

Vedas

Vishnu

Shiva, one of the Hindu Trimurti, is often shown with four hands.

Hindus seem to worship many gods. There are statues of many gods and goddesses in their shrines and places of worship. There are many stories about the different gods in their holy books. Yet Hinduism is quite clear in its teaching – there is only one God.

BRAHMAN

Hindus believe that there is only one world spirit, or God, eternal and found everywhere. This is Brahman, who takes no human form. Hindus, however, are free to imagine Brahman in any form that they find helpful.

The images that are such a feature of Hindu worship are simply showing different aspects of the whole personality of Brahman. The **atman**, or the human soul, is part of Brahman and will be reabsorbed back into God after many **reincarnations**.

A   "*There is one Ruler, the Spirit that is in all things, who transforms the one form into many… the eternal among things that pass away… whose radiance illumines all creation.*"
Katha Upanishad 5

The belief that God is to be found in all things is called **pantheism**.

THE TRIMURTI

Brahman takes three main forms:

- **Brahma – the Creator.** In the old stories, or myths, Brahma is shown as a royal figure with four heads and riding on a goose while reading the holy book of the **Vedas**. Brahma is not a popular Hindu god.

- **Vishnu – the Preserver of life.** On nine occasions Vishnu has visited Earth as an avatar, with one more to come. The most popular of the nine avatars was Krishna.

- **Shiva – the god of life, death and rebirth.** Shiva is always shown with at least four hands to show that he has power over life, death, good and evil.

TAKE TIME TO THINK

Hindus believe that everyone has an atman, a soul. Do you think that they are right? Try to explain your answer.

A STORY

There is a well-known Hindu story about a child talking to his grandmother:

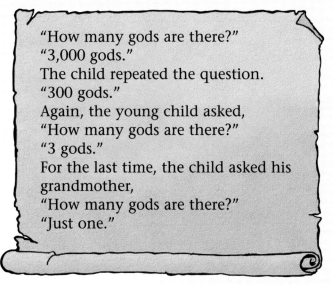

"How many gods are there?"
"3,000 gods."
The child repeated the question.
"300 gods."
Again, the young child asked,
"How many gods are there?"
"3 gods."
For the last time, the child asked his grandmother,
"How many gods are there?"
"Just one."

When you go to India, as I have done, you find that there are not many people who worship Brahma or Vishnu. Shiva, however, is different. I wear a bracelet with Shiva on it. We all have unkind or bad thoughts but Shiva helps me to banish them from my mind and that is very helpful.

Sourav, 16

OVER TO YOU ▶▶▶

1 Read through the story of the grandmother and her grandchild carefully. Sum up, in your own words, the point that you think the story is making.

2 "Hindus are not like the followers of the other great world religions. They believe in many gods." Do you think this quotation is true? Explain your answer.

3 Give two pieces of information about Brahma, Shiva and Vishnu.

GANESHA AND KRISHNA

You will find out

- About the god, Ganesha.

- About the god, Krishna.

In the glossary

Avatar

Ganesha

Bhagavad-Gita

Krishna

Shiva

Vishnu

Someone has suggested that there may be as many as 330 million gods or deities in Hinduism. If so, most of them no longer have any worshippers. Two deities, however, are very popular:

GANESHA

As you can see from the photograph, the Hindu god **Ganesha** has the head of an elephant. The holy books explain the reason for this:

Shiva was away from his consort, Parvati, for a long time. She became very lonely and, so, one day she took some mud and made the model of a boy. The boy came to life and she called him Ganesha.

While the boy was still young, his mother asked him to guard the path to the river while she went to bathe. Ganesha stood guard in the centre of the path with a sword. Shiva returned home and, not knowing who Ganesha was, tried to pass him on the path. When Ganesha tried to stop him, Shiva killed the boy by cutting off his head.

When Shiva learned the identity of the boy, he was horrified. He ordered his servant to visit Earth and bring back the first head he could find. He returned with the head of an elephant and Shiva put it on the shoulders of his son. Ganesha was saved and he is often shown in statues carrying his father's trident or with a snake around his waist.

Hindus pray to Ganesha as the god of wisdom and knowledge and, as such, he is one of the most popular Hindus deities.

Ganesha is one of the most popular Hindu gods.

Millions of Hindus identify more closely with Krishna than any of the other Hindu deities.

OVER TO **YOU** ▶▶▶

1 Copy the pictures of Ganesha and Krishna into your book and write underneath five pieces of information about each of them.

2 Copy extract A into your book and explain in your own words what you think it means.

KRISHNA

Krishna is the eighth avatar of Vishnu and he is the most popular of all the Hindu deities [A]. There are many stories about him in the Bhagavad-Gita and elsewhere.

A **""***O Krishna, blessed indeed are they who but hear of thee and meditate on this divine life and this divine play, for they become free from all worldly desires and attain to thy being. Thou art our beloved, thou art our very self.***""**

Srimad Bhagatavan 2

Krishna's parents were called Yasudev and Dewvaki. When they married, there was an evil king on the throne called Kans and he put them in prison because a wise old man had predicted that their eighth son would kill the king. The evil king killed their first six children and, when the eighth son was due, the king placed extra guards outside their prison cell.

Then a miracle happened. That night it rained very heavily and there was thunder and lightning. After the son, Krishna, was born, the prison doors were miraculously opened and the guards were put into a heavy sleep. The boy's mother carried her baby across the river and he was deposited safely in a friend's house.

The image of Krishna takes many different forms. Sometimes he is shown as a mischievous baby or as a child who spills the butter jar and eats some butter. He is also shown as a young man blowing a flute. Sometimes he is shown as a chariot driver or a warrior.

PUJA IN THE HOME

You will find out

- The five daily duties of every Hindu.

- The act of puja in the Hindu home.

- The religious responsibilities of the Hindu mother.

In the glossary

Brahmin

Ghee

Gyatri Mantra

Mandir

Mantra

Meditation

Puja

Yoga

The shrine is the centre of home life for all Hindus.

Most Hindu worship takes place in the home rather than in the **mandir**. This is mainly because Hindu society is based on the family unit and it is there that the Hindu religious traditions are safeguarded. It is in the family network that Hindu religious customs are passed down from grandparents and parents to children.

CHECK IT OUT

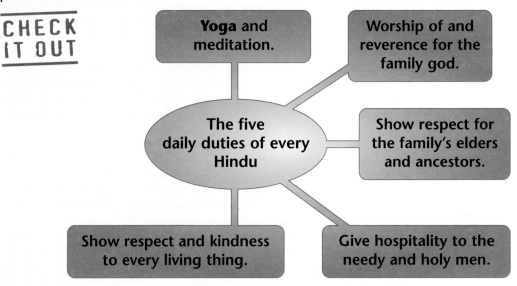

Yoga and meditation.

Worship of and reverence for the family god.

The five daily duties of every Hindu

Show respect for the family's elders and ancestors.

Show respect and kindness to every living thing.

Give hospitality to the needy and holy men.

PUJA

Puja is religious worship and this mainly takes place at home. One holy book explains that this worship can take different forms:

A *"Whatsoever form any devotee desires to worship with faith — that faith I make firm and unflinching."*

Bhagavad-Gita 7.21

Usually, this worship involves presenting offerings to the family god and chanting special words called **mantras**. Every Hindu home has its own shrine and this is treated as a very special place. Sometimes it is little more than a shelf on a wall, although the ideal is to have a whole room dedicated to the family's god. Here an image, or statue, of the god is surrounded by flowers, food and incense.

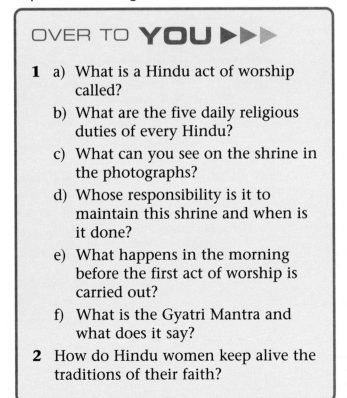

Flowers, fruit and food are renewed each day on the home shrine.

Women play a very important part in the religious ceremonies that take place in the home:

- They rise early 'to wake up' the god with a lighted candle placed in front of him or her.
- They wash the statue and wipe it all over with **ghee** [clarified butter] as a sign of respect.
- Special coloured powders are brushed onto the deity.

Sometimes the family meditates in silence. Of all the prayers that are used, the most popular is the **Gyatri Mantra** [B].

B *"Oh God! The Giver of Life, the Remover of pains and sorrows, the Bestower of happiness. Oh! Creator of the Universe. Thou art most Luminous Light, Pure and Adorable. We meditate on Thee. May we receive thy Supreme sin-destroying Light. May Thou guide our intellect in the right direction."*

Brahmins repeat the Gyatri Mantra three times a day – at dawn, at midday and at sunset. It is also used in public worship and on ceremonial occasions, such as births, marriages and the opening of important buildings.

OVER TO **YOU** ▶▶▶

1. a) What is a Hindu act of worship called?

   b) What are the five daily religious duties of every Hindu?

   c) What can you see on the shrine in the photographs?

   d) Whose responsibility is it to maintain this shrine and when is it done?

   e) What happens in the morning before the first act of worship is carried out?

   f) What is the Gyatri Mantra and what does it say?

2. How do Hindu women keep alive the traditions of their faith?

THE IMPORTANCE OF WOMEN

Women in Hindu homes have the responsibility of ensuring that the worship customs are performed properly, that the major religious festivals are kept and that their children know the great stories of their religion. In other words, it is largely the responsibility of Hindu mothers to make sure that religious traditions are handed on from one generation to the next.

TAKE TIME TO THINK

In a Hindu family, even cooking and washing up are seen as religious duties. How do you think such activities could be described as 'religious'?

THE MANDIR

Hindus meet together in a mandir [temple] to perform puja and you will find out what this involves in unit 9. For Hindus in the West, however, a mandir is much more than just a place in which to worship God. It is also the place to which Hindus come to discuss community matters as well as holding events there to raise money to help others in the worldwide Hindu community. Many mandirs also have halls in which wedding receptions are held and rooms where classes to teach adults and children about their language and religious faith are held.

MANDIRS

There are thousands of mandirs in India. Some of these buildings are huge, with beautiful and complicated designs inside and out. There are also many tiny shrines alongside roads and in the villages of India. Both kinds of building express the Hindu belief that Brahman, the Supreme Spirit, is to be found everywhere and takes on many different forms.

Hindus believe that a mandir is a house where a deity or deities live. Each mandir is dedicated to Shiva, Vishnu or Shakti, the mother goddess. Some mandirs, however, house all three of these deities, together with **Hanuman** and Ganesha. The main shrine in the mandir has the image or **murti** to whom the mandir is dedicated. Surrounding shrines often hold the murtis of other deities.

In the West, a mandir is usually a converted house or church. Sometimes, however, purpose-built mandirs are put up in areas which have a large Hindu population. One such mandir is situated in Neasdon, in London, the largest mandir to be found outside India.

SYMBOLS IN THE MANDIR

Most mandirs have many, if not all, of these symbols. They have important symbolic meanings for Hindu worshippers:

CHECK
IT OUT

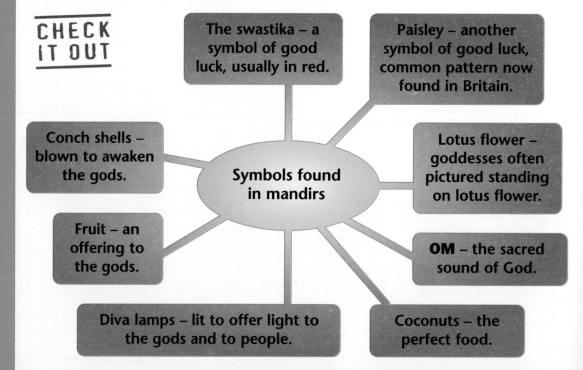

The swastika – a symbol of good luck, usually in red.

Paisley – another symbol of good luck, common pattern now found in Britain.

Conch shells – blown to awaken the gods.

Lotus flower – goddesses often pictured standing on lotus flower.

Symbols found in mandirs

Fruit – an offering to the gods.

OM – the sacred sound of God.

Diva lamps – lit to offer light to the gods and to people.

Coconuts – the perfect food.

VISITING A MANDIR

If you were to visit a mandir, you would take off your shoes and walk up some steps and under a carved arch. As you walk inside, you would see the murti directly in front of you – they are at the far end of the building, under a pyramid-shaped tower. You would smell incense and ghee burning. On your way out, you would be given **prashad**, holy food, to eat.

A wayside shrine in India. Many of them are tiny.

TAKE TIME TO THINK

Some Hindus make regular visits to a mandir while others scarcely do at all. What do you think a Hindu might get of spiritual value from paying a regular visit to the mandir?

OVER TO **YOU** ▶▶▶

1   Make a list of the other uses to which a mandir is put apart from being used as a place of worship.

2   Find out as much as you can about four of the symbols often found in a mandir and draw them in your book.

3   Explain what a murti is and say why you will find one of them, or more, in a mandir.

Inside a Hindu temple.

19

IN THE MANDIR

You will find out

- About acts of puja in a mandir.
- About the tilak mark.

In the glossary

Arti

Bhajan

Ghee

Havan

Mandir

Tilak

Not everyone worships in a mandir, but many do.

Hindu temples, or mandirs, are usually built at places where, according to tradition, a god has appeared or lived on Earth. Some of the temples built on these sites are large, spacious and beautiful. Others are scarcely large enough to contain a priest and an image of the god.

WORSHIP IN THE MANDIR

Most mandirs have at least one priest. He looks after the image of the god and helps the people to worship in an appropriate way. The people do not worship the image but the god of which the image is a symbol. To do so, they usually arrive early in the morning and:

- Ring the bell-rope to announce their arrival for worship.
- Take off their shoes as they enter the mandir as a sign of their respect for the god.
- Present their offerings of food, flowers, milk or honey to the priest, who takes them into the shrine-room to be laid before the god.
- After receiving the offerings, the priest offers prayers in front of the people. These are made up of three parts:

1. Bhajans

These are devotional hymns or songs. Musical instruments are played to accompany them and worshippers clap their hands to accompany the singing. This music is an important part of Hindu worship.

Dancing is another popular form of worship. Travelling groups of dancers often perform the most well-known stories from the Hindu scriptures and this helps people in village areas to remember them.

2. Havan

This involves making an offering of fire to the god. To do this, the priest lights a small fire in front of the image using wood and ghee.

3. Arti

This is a ceremony during which love and devotion are offered to the god. A small tray containing five lights is waved in front of the statue of the god. It is then taken to the worshippers, who run their hands over the flames before wiping their hands on their head. Hindus believe that, when they do this, they receive power from their god.

A *"Whatever a zealous soul may offer,*
Be it a leaf, a flower, fruit or water,
That I willingly accept
For it was given in love."

The god Krishna in the Bhagavad-Gita

TAKE TIME TO THINK

Read the words of the god Krishna in extract A. What important point do you think he is making about worship?

TILAK

During the worship in the mandir, people place a dot or stripes of a special powder on their foreheads. This is the **tilak**, which indicates that a person has been to worship. The tilak is not to be confused with the red dot that Hindu women place on their foreheads to show that they are married.

OVER TO YOU ▶▶▶

1 Make a list of reasons why Hindus may want to worship in a mandir.

2 "What is the point of making an offering to God when everything belongs to God anyway?" Discuss this question with your partner and report back to your class.

3 "Dancing has nothing to do with religion." How might a Hindu answer this statement?

The mark on this Hindu woman's forehead shows that she has been to the mandir to worship.

REACHING MOKSHA

The hope of every Hindu is that he or she will reach moksha. This is the state of spiritual freedom from the cycle of birth – death – rebirth.

Hindus believe that the soul of each person is given a new body with each rebirth and this happens many times before moksha is reached. Eventually, the soul is reunited with Brahman. The Bhagavad-Gita mentions four ways in which this can be achieved:

THE PATH OF KNOWLEDGE – JNANA YOGA

This path is the most difficult for anyone to take to liberation. Not only does it require constant guidance from a spiritual teacher [a guru] but also the ability to understand all of the Hindu scriptures - an impossible task. Only a few people have been able to free themselves from attachment to the world through a complete knowledge of the scriptures.

THE PATH OF DEVOTION – BHAKTI YOGA

This path includes a person choosing a particular god or goddess and spending the whole of their life in devotion to them. This means:

CHECK IT OUT

Praying to the god or goddess.

Trying to remember the god or goddess at all times.

The path of devotion involves…

Serving others in the name of the god or goddess.

Offering daily worship at the shrine of the god or goddess.

Hymn singing, telling the stories of the gods, religious drama, celebrating the religious festivals and pilgrimages are all part of the bhakti tradition.

THE PATH OF GOOD ACTIONS – KARMA YOGA

According to the Bhagavad-Gita, the moral law which governs the whole of life is that good deeds bear good fruit and bad deeds bad fruit. This is cause and effect. The way that a person lives in one life affects the level at which they return in the next. This is called the law of **karma**.

Everything that a person does, including sleeping, working, eating and speaking, affects their karma. Every human being, therefore, must take particular care to only do those actions which produce good karma as all actions affect their next reincarnation. They do this by doing their **dharma** – their duties – to the best of their ability.

Practising yoga.

THE PATH OF MEDITATION

Yoga is a series of physical and mental exercises designed to give a person control over their body and mind. A person who practises yoga is called a yogi [male] or a yogini [female]. The ancient Hindu holy books set out a number of requirements for any who would practise yoga successfully. They must have self-control, non-violence, truthfulness, chastity and avoid greed. To do this they must master certain postures – the most important of which is the 'lotus position'.

No path is better than the others. Hindus liken the path to moksha to climbing a mountain – the chosen path does not matter, although some paths to the summit are steeper than others.

A *"Whatever you do, eat, offer as an oblation, give as a gift or undertake as a penance, offer all that to me."*

Lord Krishna

TAKE TIME TO THINK

Why do you think that many Hindus feel that the pathway of actions is the easiest one for them to follow to moksha.

OVER TO YOU ▶▶▶

1 Describe, in your own words, the pathway of devotion.

2 a) Look at extract A. Which path is this quotation suggesting that Hindus should follow?

   b) Write three sentences to explain what following this pathway involves.

The teachings of Hinduism try to provide answers to some of the most important questions of life:

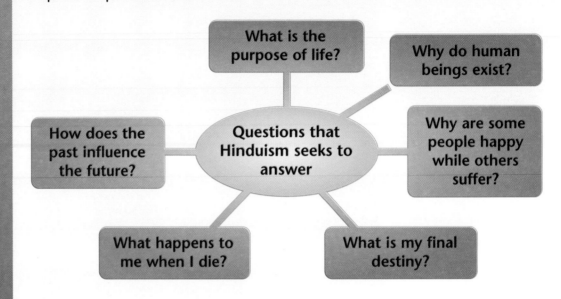

The answers to these questions are found in three Hindu beliefs:

SAMSARA

Samsara means 'wandering' and refers to the wandering of the soul from body to body, in one lifetime after another. It is the cycle that everyone passes through – birth, death and rebirth. You can also see it in nature. The trees die each winter only for new buds to appear the following spring [A].

> A *"For sure is the death of all that is born, sure is the birth of all that dies; so in a matter that no one can prevent, you have no cause to grieve."*
>
> Bhagavad-Gita 2.27

Hindus believe that even the universe goes through the same process. The universe has come into existence many times, disintegrated and then reformed again.

KARMA

Karma means 'action'. The law of karma means the law of cause and effect. Hindus believe that they have been reborn many times. The effect of their actions in the past are carried forward each time they are reborn. Bad actions in a past life lead to suffering in the present existence. Unselfish actions in the past lead to a happy life in the present.

Nothing happens by accident. Everything that happens to a person in this life comes about because of something they have done. This means that people can influence their destiny in the future. It also explains why people enjoy happy or unhappy lives.

MOKSHA

Although many Hindus hope for a good rebirth in the next life, this is not their final goal. Above everything, they hope that their soul, atman, will escape samsara altogether. A famous prayer from one of the Hindu holy books describes moksha in this way:

B *"From the unreal lead me to the real,*
   From darkness lead me to light,
   From death lead me to immortality"
                    Brihadaranyka Upanishad 1.iii.28

The Hindu holy books describe moksha in different ways:

OVER TO YOU ▶▶▶

1 "A belief in karma helps Hindus to accept any suffering they might experience in this life." Do you agree with this?

2 Explain the meaning of these three words in your own words:
   a) Samsara
   b) Karma
   c) Moksha

Perfect peace.

Perfect happiness.

The bliss of union with God.

Moksha is...

The soul losing itself in Brahman.

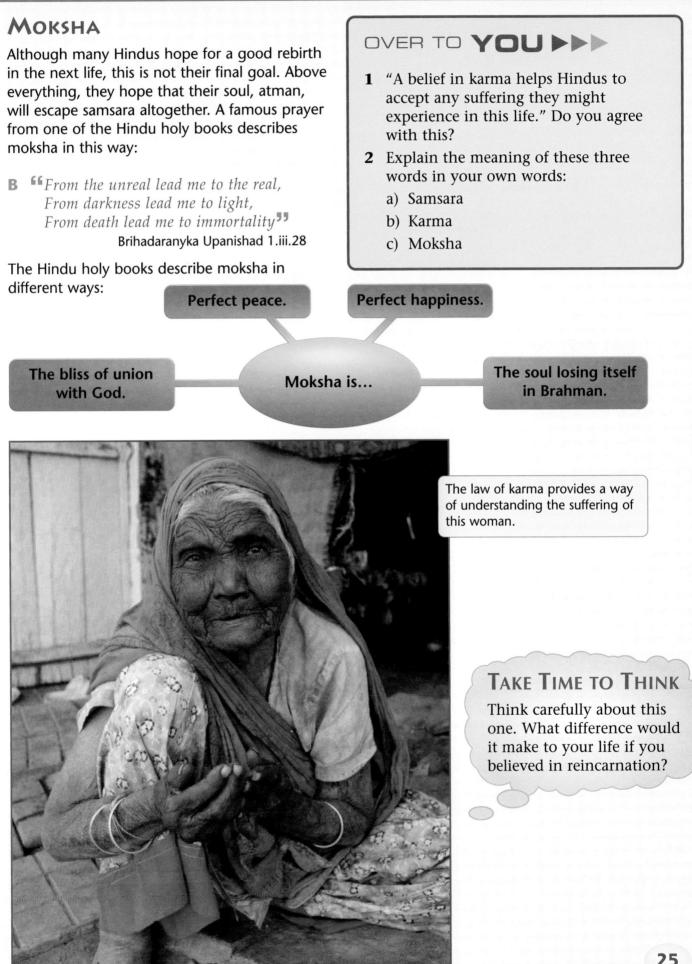

The law of karma provides a way of understanding the suffering of this woman.

TAKE TIME TO THINK

Think carefully about this one. What difference would it make to your life if you believed in reincarnation?

THE SAMSKARAS

You will find out

- The meaning of 'rites of passage'.

- The sixteen samskaras of Hinduism and their importance.

In the glossary

Caste System

Karma

Laws of Manu

Sacred Thread

Samskara

Sannyasin

Pregnancy is a very worrying time for mothers-to-be in India and three samskaras are carried out before the baby is born.

RITES OF PASSAGE

Rites of passage are special ceremonies in different religions which mark the transition from one stage of life to another. These ceremonies are mainly concerned with birth, reaching adulthood, getting married and death. These ceremonies are deeply personal and emotional as well as being important to society.

Rites of passage are celebrated during public gatherings of friends and relatives. In Hinduism, these rites of passage are called **samskaras**. In the Sanskrit language, this word means 'being made fit for use', just as cooking makes food fit to eat. Going through a samskara ensures that the person is fit to go on to the next stage in their life.

TAKE TIME TO THINK

Why do you think that all cultures and societies have 'rites of passage' to mark the different stages that people pass through?

OVER TO YOU ▶▶▶

1 What do you think are the five most important times in your life? Write them down in your book. Compare your list with your partner. What do you think is the most appropriate way to celebrate each of the events on your list?

2 a) Explain in your own words what a samskara is.

   b) How many samskaras are there in Hinduism?

   c) Name some of the events in a person's life that are covered by the different samskaras.

THE SIXTEEN SAMSKARAS

Sixteen samskaras are described in the Hindu holy books. They mark all of the important stages in a person's life. They are said to be a religious duty in the important **Laws of Manu** – an ancient book of Hindu laws.

Not all sixteen of the samskaras will be fully observed by every Hindu. They will, however, be recognised in some way. They are:

1.   This ceremony is celebrated at the first menstruation of a new bride to wish for her to conceive and bring a new baby into the world.

2/3.   Special rituals performed during pregnancy at the 2nd or 3rd month and the 6th or 8th month to make sure that the baby is developing properly.

4.   Birth ceremony.

5.   Naming ceremony.

6.   The child's first outing at 4 months.

7.   The child taking its first solid food.

8.   The child's first haircut between 1 and 3 years. This is a purifying ceremony to remove the child's previous karma.

9.   Child's ears are pierced.

10.   The sacred thread ceremony [unit 15]. This is the initiation of boys from the upper three castes into the student stage of life [unit 4].

11.   The start of a child's education.

12.   Graduation from studies.

13.   Marriage [unit 16].

14.   Retirement [unit 4]. This usually takes place around the age of 60.

15.   Withdrawing from worldly concerns and becoming a holy man [**sannyasin**]. This is supposed to take place at the age of 75 but can, in practice, take place earlier or later.

16.   Death rites [unit 17]. This will also include ceremonies which pay respect to relatives who have already died.

SAMSKARAS BEFORE AND AFTER BIRTH

You will find out

- The early samskaras that are carried out before a baby is born.

- The 4th and 5th samskaras that are performed soon after a baby is born.

- The 5th samskara, when a child is given its name.

In the glossary

Ashrama

Ghee

Karma

Mantra

Samskara

Sacred Syllable

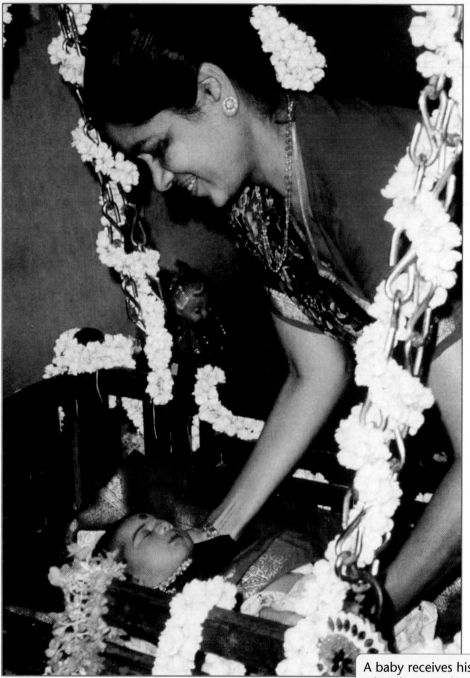

A baby receives his name when he is twelve days old.

Many Hindus believe that life is like a journey. As they make their way through life, they must be careful to choose the correct path and make sure that they do not collect any bad karma on the way. Each samskara which is performed helps them on this journey.

Hindus also believe that each of the four ashramas [unit 4] should last for 25 years. This means that everyone, if they live properly, can expect to reach their 100th birthday before they die.

THE EARLY SAMSKARAS

The first samskara takes place when a woman has married, as she hopes for conception, and the couple pray about the kind of baby they would like. The second and the third samskaras are intended to give protection to the baby and strength to the mother.

THE FOURTH AND FIFTH SAMSKARAS

When the baby is born, he or she is washed and then the father places a few drops of honey or ghee into their mouth, using a gold ring. The 4th samskara takes place soon after the baby is born. The **sacred syllable** [unit 8] is written on the baby's tongue using a golden pen dipped in honey. This is the syllable that begins all prayers, so it is like saying that the baby's whole life will be like a prayer. The father then recites a prayer taken from the Hindu scriptures.

Another samskara is performed 11 days later, when the baby receives its name. In Hinduism, the choice of name is very important since the right name can bring good fortune on the child throughout its lifetime.

In fact, at this time, the child is often given two names:

- The public name by which he or she will be known by others.

- The secret name by which he or she will only be known during special religious occasions.

The baby receives its names in a very simple way. The father just leans over a baby and whispers in its ear, "Your name is…" The father then repeats a series of mantras in which he asks that the child might receive strength, understanding and wisdom. He also asks that his son or daughter might be protected from evil spirits.

A *"May God the creator of all things grant you firm wisdom. Knowledge and wisdom are the sources of power and long life."*

In devout Hindu families, the ceremony is carried out by the priest in the temple but, in most families, it is performed in the baby's home. The baby's name is announced by the oldest woman in the family while the other women sing songs to the baby. All of the married women are given a handful of cooked pulses, such as chick peas, together with light refreshments.

TAKE TIME TO THINK

Hindu families place a very great importance on the name that they choose for their son or daughter. Why do you think it is so important to them?

OVER TO YOU ▶▶▶

1 What is the significance of the sacred syllable being written on the tongue of the baby with a golden pen dipped in honey?

2 Why do you think that a special sweet made of fruits, nuts and sugar is given to friends and relatives who attend the naming of a Hindu baby?

3 Hindu children are often given the same names as a god or a goddess. Why do you think Hindu parents do this?

FAMILY LIFE

Hindu children undergo several samskaras before they reach adulthood.

The vast majority of people in the world live in either:

- A **nuclear family** with parents and children.

or

- An **extended family**, which has three or more generations including grandparents, aunts and uncles, living together in the same household.

Hindus, as we will see in unit 16, see marriage as the coming together of two families, with the extended families giving their support and help. Within this framework, everyone has their particular responsibilities and this is how they work out their dharma.

GROWING UP

As we saw in unit 12, there are sixteen samskaras – rituals that mark the different stages in a person's life. Twelve of these samskaras take place before and shortly after birth or during childhood. The extent to which they are kept, and the ways that each is celebrated, varies from one tradition [jati] or caste to another. Many families just concentrate on two or three of them.

THE FAMILY SHRINE

As we saw in unit 7, the family shrine plays a very important role in the life of most Hindus. It may be grand or very modest, but it is the focal point for an everyday act of worship in which every family member is expected to play a part. During the act of puja, food is offered to the murti and this becomes prashad or holy food. Each person accepts this as a gift of God's grace.

> I spend some time in front of the shrine in my house each day. I find that this gives me a sense of peace that I then carry with me into the day ahead. Sometimes I take part in an act of worship with members of my family and sometimes I just spend time there alone.
>
> Mina, 17

THE ELDERLY

Traditionally, the stage of retirement is the third ashrama and responsibility for looking after the family passes to the next generation. The elderly now have the time to do other things:

CHECK IT OUT

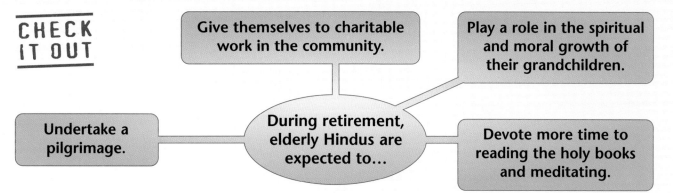

Give themselves to charitable work in the community.

Play a role in the spiritual and moral growth of their grandchildren.

Undertake a pilgrimage.

During retirement, elderly Hindus are expected to…

Devote more time to reading the holy books and meditating.

A small number of male Hindus take the duties of the fourth ashrama on board and give up all worldly attachments. They become known as Sannyasins.

It is Hindu teaching that the needs of elderly people should be looked after in the extended family. However, in Britain, this is often impossible, as children leave the area and the elderly live alone. One society, Navjivan, now exists to look after the needs of elderly Asian people – providing them with vegetarian meals, transport and different social activities.

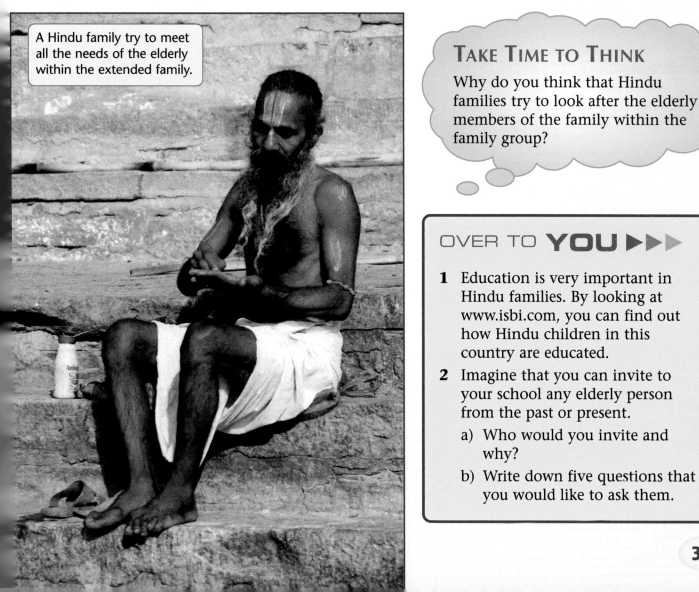

A Hindu family try to meet all the needs of the elderly within the extended family.

TAKE TIME TO THINK

Why do you think that Hindu families try to look after the elderly members of the family within the family group?

OVER TO YOU ▶▶▶

1 Education is very important in Hindu families. By looking at www.isbi.com, you can find out how Hindu children in this country are educated.

2 Imagine that you can invite to your school any elderly person from the past or present.
   a) Who would you invite and why?
   b) Write down five questions that you would like to ask them.

THE SACRED THREAD CEREMONY

Most religions mark the transition from being a child to being an adult with a special ceremony. In Hinduism, boys from the Brahmin, **Kshatriya** and Vaishya castes receive their sacred thread and are known as 'twice-born'. They can now enter fully into the adult duties and responsibilities of their caste.

RECEIVING THE SACRED THREAD

Several important things take place during this, the 10th samskara:

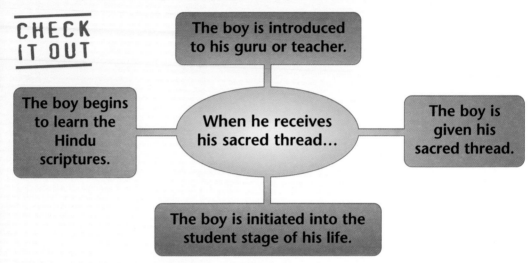

CHECK IT OUT

The boy is introduced to his guru or teacher.

The boy begins to learn the Hindu scriptures.

When he receives his sacred thread...

The boy is given his sacred thread.

The boy is initiated into the student stage of his life.

THE SACRED THREAD

The sacred thread consists of three threads. These symbolise the three promises which every young Hindu adult is expected to make and follow during his life:

- The obligation to pass on the knowledge that he learns from the wise men of the past and the scientists of the present.
- The obligation to look after and respect his parents and ancestors.
- The obligation towards the community in which he lives and the wider Hindu community.

OVER TO **YOU** ▶▶▶

1   a) Why do you think that members of the three highest castes who go through the ceremony are called 'twice-born'.

    b) Why do you think that members of the lowest caste do not undergo the ceremony.

2   Imagine that you have been sent along to cover a sacred thread ceremony in your local temple. Describe what happens during the ceremony.

3   Astrologers play a part in many Hindu ceremonies. Many people who are not Hindus read their horoscopes in newspapers and magazines. Do you think that a person's 'star-sign' has any importance? Talk about it with your partner.

THE SACRED THREAD CEREMONY

The best day to hold the sacred thread ceremony is usually chosen by the priest or an astrologer. Then:

- The boy's head is shaved, apart from a tuft of hair on the crown.
- The boy takes a bath and wears a special white dhoti.
- The boy stands facing west, opposite his father, who is facing east. A piece of cloth is held between the father and son and songs of blessing are sung.
- The priest conducts a special fire ritual. Agni is the Hindu god of fire and rice and ghee are offered up.
- The boy is given new clothes and a loop of white cotton is placed across his left shoulder. The father then says:

"May this sacred thread destroy my ignorance, grant me long life and increase my understanding."

and his son repeats the words.
- The boy will wear the sacred thread day and night for the rest of his life. It will be renewed annually.

TAKE TIME TO THINK

How do you think the sacred thread ceremony might affect a Hindu boy's attitude to his life and his family?

This Hindu boy will wear his sacred thread for the rest of his life.

CHECK IT OUT

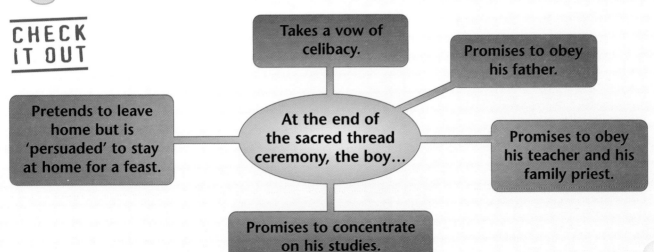

Takes a vow of celibacy.

Promises to obey his father.

Pretends to leave home but is 'persuaded' to stay at home for a feast.

At the end of the sacred thread ceremony, the boy...

Promises to obey his teacher and his family priest.

Promises to concentrate on his studies.

MARRIAGE AND DIVORCE

The 13th samskara is reached when a Hindu marries and becomes a householder. The first ashrama, the stage of the student, has been completed. Now, during the second ashrama, the Hindu sets himself three religious aims:

- To build up some merit in the hope that he can avoid being reborn.
- To achieve wealth.
- To enjoy real pleasure.

PREPARATION FOR MARRIAGE

Most Hindu marriages are arranged by parents. In India, girls are allowed to marry at 18 while boys have to wait three years longer. Hindus living elsewhere, however, are bound by the laws of the country in which they live. When choosing a suitable marriage partner for their son or daughter, Hindu parents bear in mind:

- Both men and women must come from the same caste.
- A horoscope must be drawn up for the man and the woman to see if they are compatible.

THE WEDDING CLOTHES

A Hindu bride is prepared carefully for her wedding. Henna is painted on her hands and feet. A tilak [a red spot] is painted in the middle of her forehead to show that she has been blessed by God.

This Hindu couple are tied together in their wedding ceremony.

In India, the traditional wedding outfit for the bride to wear is a red **sari** trimmed with gold, supplemented by gold jewellery. The groom can either wear a 'kurta-pajana' [a long, loose-fitting top with trousers] or a Western style suit.

THE WEDDING CEREMONY

The actual wedding ceremony is carried out by a priest and takes place, as do many Hindu ceremonies, around a holy fire. This symbolises the presence and blessing of God. The priest keeps the fire burning throughout the ceremony by pouring ghee onto the flames. He also throws rice and spices on the fire since these are traditional Hindu symbols of fertility.

The bride's parents give her to the groom by placing her hand in his. A cord is then placed around the groom's neck while the other end is attached to the bride's sari. Together the couple take seven steps around the sacred fire as prayers are said. The seven steps represent:

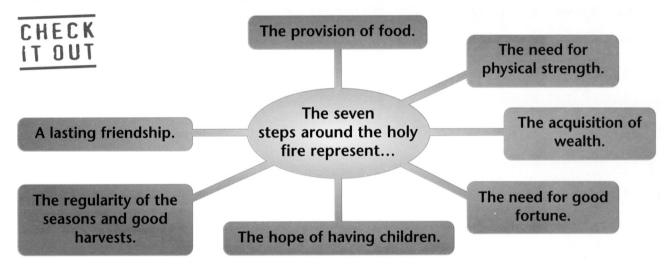

CHECK
IT OUT

The seven steps around the holy fire represent…

- The provision of food.
- The need for physical strength.
- The acquisition of wealth.
- A lasting friendship.
- The need for good fortune.
- The regularity of the seasons and good harvests.
- The hope of having children.

While taking the seven steps, the man says to the woman:

A **"**With utmost love to each other we walk together… May we make our minds united, of the same vows and of the same thoughts. I am the wind and you are the melody. I am the melody and you are the words. Into my will I take thy heart. Thy heart shall follow mine. And the heart of mine be yours.**"**

DIVORCE

Strict Hindus believe that marriage is for life although, in India, the law does allow divorce. Hindu families look upon divorce as a great disgrace for both families.

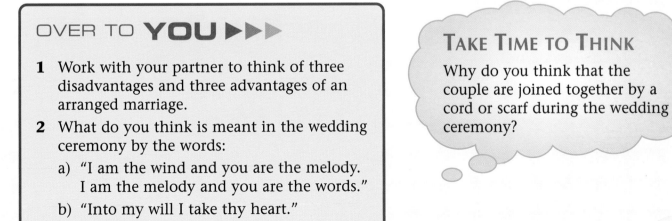

OVER TO **YOU** ▶▶▶

1 Work with your partner to think of three disadvantages and three advantages of an arranged marriage.
2 What do you think is meant in the wedding ceremony by the words:
   a) "I am the wind and you are the melody. I am the melody and you are the words."
   b) "Into my will I take thy heart."

TAKE TIME TO THINK

Why do you think that the couple are joined together by a cord or scarf during the wedding ceremony?

After the 14th samskara [the third ashrama], which is retirement from work, and the 15th samskara [the fourth ashrama], which is a turning away from all that is worldly, only one samskara remains: that is death, followed by cremation.

THE HINDU FUNERAL CEREMONY

Hindu tradition only allows holy men and babies to be buried. Otherwise the corpse is reduced to ashes by burning [cremation]. A burial-ground is to be found outside most Indian villages. There the bodies are burned beneath a covering of wood, usually sandalwood.

- The cremation takes place on the same day as death, before sunset.

- As soon as death is confirmed, the body is washed and dressed by relatives.

- The body is carried in procession to the cremation ground on a stretcher, covered by a simple cloth – to emphasise that everyone, rich and poor, is equal in death.

- The dead person's eldest son leads the procession. On the way home, it is led by the youngest son.

- The eldest son walks three times round the body, pours holy water over it and puts a flame to the wood. As he does so, he says:

A *"I apply fire to all the limits of the person who, willingly or unwillingly, might have committed lapses and is now under the clutches of death – a person attended with virtue and vice, greed and ignorance. May he attain the shining regions."*

A constant supply of ghee is thrown on the flames to keep them alight. Dry pieces of sugar cane are also squeezed between the splints of sandalwood.

The eldest son breaks the skull of the dead person with a stick to release their soul.

OVER TO YOU ▶▶▶

1 Why do Hindus hope to be able to scatter the ashes of a loved one on the waters of the River Ganges?

2 Why does the eldest son crack open the skull of the dead person?

3 What takes place in the Hindu funeral ceremony to underline the belief that everyone is equal in death?

4 Read extract B. What do you think the Bhagavad-Gita means when it talks of the "embodied soul"?

AFTER THE CREMATION

On the day after the cremation, the eldest son collects the bones and ashes and scatters them over the waters of the nearest river. Hindus believe that anyone who has their ashes scattered on the waters of the sacred river, the River Ganges, escapes future rebirths.

Ten days of important religious ceremonies follow. During this time:

- The eldest son offers rice and milk each day in case the soul of the dead person returns to haunt his or her family.

- The relatives visit the eldest son on the 4th day to comfort the family and give them presents. They also offer up prayers for the dead person.

- A final meeting of sympathy is held on the 11th day and this is the time when the soul of the dead person is free to find another body in which to dwell.

You can see how the Bhagavad-Gita explains this in extract B:

B "*As a man puts off his worn out clothes*
And puts on new ones,
So the embodied soul puts off worn-out bodies
And goes to others that are new."

Bhagavad-Gita

TAKE TIME TO THINK
Why do you think that Hindus see death as a time for hope as well as sadness?

Scenes like this are a common sight in India, close to any of its rivers. This one is on the shore of the River Ganges.

THE HOLY TEXTS

There are a large number of sacred writings in Hinduism. These are used:

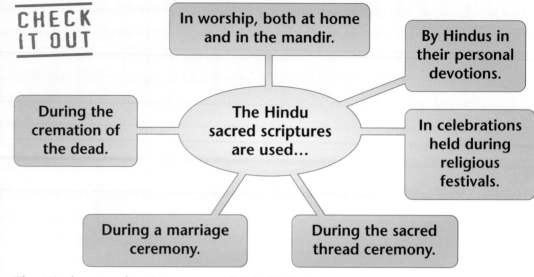

CHECK IT OUT

In worship, both at home and in the mandir.

By Hindus in their personal devotions.

During the cremation of the dead.

The Hindu sacred scriptures are used...

In celebrations held during religious festivals.

During a marriage ceremony.

During the sacred thread ceremony.

The Hindu sacred scriptures are divided into two groups:

THE SHRUTI

The word **Shruti** means 'that which is heard'. This refers to those writings which are believed to have been composed by God. They are thought to contain an accurate record of the words spoken by God. These words were remembered, and written down, by the sages and holy men of the past. They were then passed on word for word and so are completely accurate and reliable.

You can see from the illustration which of the sacred scriptures belong to this group of books. The contents of these books have remained the same for thousands of years. Hindus believe that the words of God must not be altered or changed in any way.

The Vedas are the most important examples of Shruti. They are arranged under four headings and each of these has four parts. They mainly contain prayers and songs, called mantras, as well as sections written specially for hermits who live isolated lives in forests.

THE SMRITI

The word **Smriti** means 'those that can be remembered'. These are books which are believed to have been written by those people who have already reached moksha and were put together between about 200 BCE and 200 CE. These books contain the words that people can 'remember' having been told about God rather than the words of God.

Hindus disagree among themselves as to how important these books are. The contents of these books have changed over time and continue to change to make the books apply to the lives of Hindus today.

Most Hindus do not mind that the contents of these books have changed. They reply that the purpose of the books is to help them understand their relationship with God and this group contains most of the best-loved sacred books in Hinduism. It does not matter as long as the spiritual message of the books remains the same.

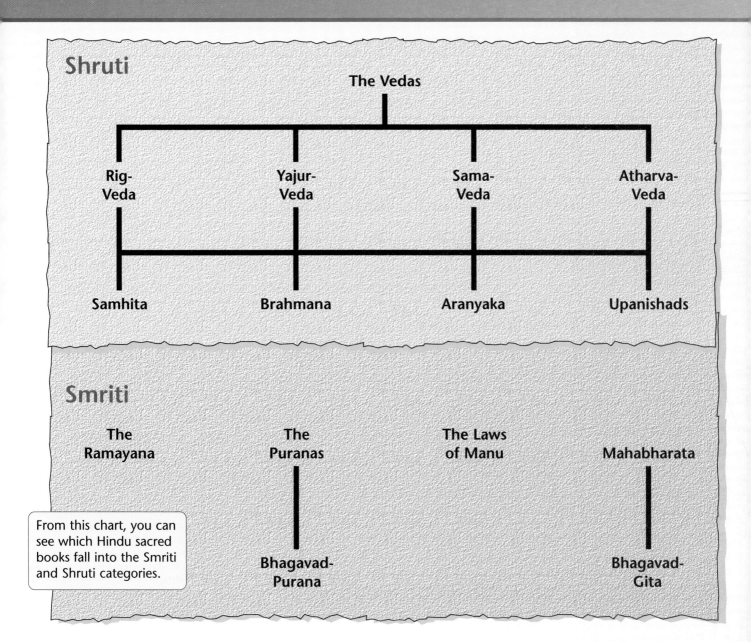

Shruti

The Vedas

Rig-Veda | Yajur-Veda | Sama-Veda | Atharva-Veda

Samhita | Brahmana | Aranyaka | Upanishads

Smriti

The Ramayana | The Puranas | The Laws of Manu | Mahabharata

Bhagavad-Purana | | | Bhagavad-Gita

From this chart, you can see which Hindu sacred books fall into the Smriti and Shruti categories.

OVER TO **YOU** ▶▶▶

1 a) What do the words 'Shruti' and 'Smriti' mean?

   b) What is the difference between the two different groups of books?

   c) How is the attitude of Hindus different towards the two groups of books?

2 How reliable do you think the memory is? Would you be prepared to trust the memories of others when it came to belief in God?

3 a) Describe your memory of something that happened to you when you were much younger.

   b) Do you think that your description of this event is absolutely reliable in all its details?

TAKE TIME TO THINK

In the earliest times, the sacred stories and legends of Hinduism were kept alive and passed around by word of mouth before they were written down. Can you think of two advantages and two disadvantages of keeping material alive in this way for a long time?

THE SACREDNESS OF LIFE

You will find out

- About Hinduism and the sacredness of life.

- The Hindu belief that all forms of life are related to each other.

- The Hindu belief in rebirth.

In the glossary

Bhagavad-Gita

Brahman

Brahmin

Guru

Hindus believe that human beings have a responsibility for every other part of nature.

Among the most important aspects of religion are the ways that it affects the way that people live; their outlook on life; the attitude that they have towards other people and the different ways in which religious people affect the society in which they live. There is a direct link between the quality of life in any community and the religious life that the majority of people follow.

HINDUISM AND THE SACREDNESS OF LIFE

The Hindu scriptures and the moral codes that Hindus follow strongly teach that all life is sacred. This includes:

- Human life.
- Animal life.
- Plant life.

There is a simple reason for this. Hinduism teaches that the universal spirit [Brahman] is to be found in everything that exists in the universe. In other words, God is the creator of all that exists and is to be found in everything. This means that everything that exists is sacred or holy. This is how one of the Hindu holy books describes this:

A *"His Being is the source of all beings, the seed of all things that are in this life have their life in God. He is God hidden in all beings, their inmost soul. He lives in all things and watches all things."*

Svetasvatara Upanishad 1.16

EVERYONE IS RELATED

Hindus believe that everything in the world, both living beings [human beings, animals] and inanimate matter [rocks, mountains, trees, etc] are an expression of God. Living beings are connected to and dependent on one another. The Bhagavad-Gita teaches that it is only the holy man, the guru, who is wise enough to see this. He is one with Brahman since he is free from all sin. The wise man lives in God and God lives in the wise man.

REBIRTH

The belief in rebirth means that, in some way, everyone is related to all living beings. Your dog may have been your sister in a previous life! Hindus also believe that all living beings are different forms of God so they should respect all forms of life, whether it is animal or human, rich or poor; born into a high or a low family, powerful or powerless. This extract from the Bhagavad-Gita makes this clear:

B *"On a Brahmin full of knowledge and good conduct, on a cow, on a dog, or on a person of unclean caste, wise men look with equal eye."*

Bhagavad-Gita

As we shall see, the Hindu belief in the sacredness of life and the interconnectedness of all beings affects the Hindu attitude to a whole range of issues considered in this book. In particular:

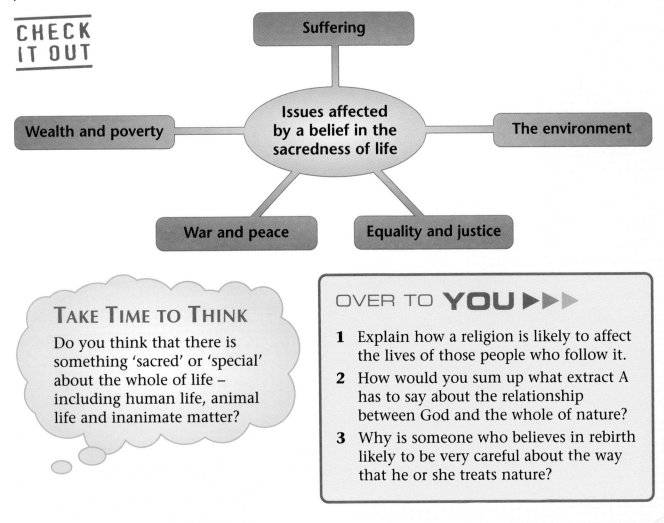

CHECK IT OUT

Suffering

Wealth and poverty

Issues affected by a belief in the sacredness of life

The environment

War and peace

Equality and justice

TAKE TIME TO THINK

Do you think that there is something 'sacred' or 'special' about the whole of life – including human life, animal life and inanimate matter?

OVER TO YOU ▶▶▶

1 Explain how a religion is likely to affect the lives of those people who follow it.

2 How would you sum up what extract A has to say about the relationship between God and the whole of nature?

3 Why is someone who believes in rebirth likely to be very careful about the way that he or she treats nature?

WEALTH AND POVERTY

You will find out

- The four aims in life for every Hindu.

- The importance of acquiring wealth.

- The Hindu teaching on money.

In the glossary

Artha

Ashrama

Dharma

Kama

Mahabharata

Moksha

Hindus believe that there are four worthy aims in life for everyone:

Four worthy aims in life for all Hindus

- Dharma – to keep to one's religious and social duty.
- **Artha** – to gain wealth by any legitimate means.
- **Kama** – to enjoy the good things in life.
- Moksha – to enjoy final freedom or liberation at the end of life.

ACQUIRING WEALTH

Hinduism is the only religion that lays down the acquisition of wealth as a worthy aim in life. Although acquiring wealth is a worthy aim in life, however, it must not be allowed to dominate a person's life. It is important because, in the second stage of life [ashrama], the householder phase, a man must support many people – his children, his wife and his older relatives [A].

> **A** *"Puffed up with self-conceit, unbending,*
> *Filled with the madness and pride of wealth,*
> *They offer sacrifices that are but sacrifices in name*
> *And not in the way prescribed – the hypocrites!"*
>
> Bhagavad-Gita 16.17

In Hinduism, the wealth that a person has does not belong to him alone. It belongs to his whole family. In Indian society, this means four living generations and three generations of ancestors. The present generation enjoying the wealth are trustees for other generations to come. They are expected to look after it carefully.

After they have met their family obligations, Hindus are expected to give away the wealth that they do not need. This is why begging is such a strong Hindu tradition. It gives people with wealth the opportunity to gain merit in the next life by giving some of their wealth to those in need.

THE HINDU TEACHING ABOUT MONEY

During the Hindu wedding ceremony, the bridegroom promises his father-in-law three times that he will always follow dharma, artha and kama 'in moderation'. This moderation is important. Hindus must never be greedy. They must not be preoccupied with making money. If they are, their family will suffer.

From this, Hindus learn that there are more important things in life than making money. The Hindu holy books point out what these things are:

- To obtain wisdom.
- To love God.
- To carry out family responsibilities to the best of their ability.

All of these are much more important than having money.

TAKE TIME TO THINK

Make a list of the three most important aims that you think human beings should have in life. Are all of them more important to you than making money?

Hinduism strongly makes the point that a person's main obligation is to members of his own family.

THE MAHABHARATA

The **Mahabharata** is the longest poem in the world and a much-loved Hindu holy book. It teaches that the way a person lives is much more important than the wealth they have. Having money should lead to generosity and compassion. It should give a person a great desire to celebrate the religious ceremonies. It should result in pleasure, courage, self-confidence, learning and joy. These are all spiritual qualities that make a person better.

OVER TO **YOU** ▶▶▶

1 Write four sentences about the Hindu attitude to wealth. In particular, mention the obligation that having wealth places on a person.

2 Why do Hindus believe that begging is an important spiritual activity?

3 Discuss with your partner and make a list of some of the ways that a Hindu might feel that they should not make money.

PROPER AND IMPROPER OCCUPATIONS FOR HINDUS

You will find out

- The right and wrong ways for Hindus to earn money.

- How Hindus can earn money honestly.

- The bad ways for Hindus to become rich.

In the glossary

Ashrama

Caste System

Dharma

Karma

Hindus believe that wealth is a good thing but only if it has been obtained by lawful means. Other people must not be hurt by the way that a person earns their money. If people follow their dharma [social duty] in the ashrama [stage in life] and this allows them to become rich then they should enjoy it. People must do the right job for the caste to which they belong.

THE UNEQUAL DISTRIBUTION OF WEALTH

In Hindu society, in India, wealth is distributed very unevenly. At one end of the scale are the very wealthy who can spend money as they wish. At the other end of the scale are people who live in such poverty that their only home is on the street of a large town. For them a banana or biscuit is considered a great luxury.

Poverty as great as this can lead people to gain money by any means – often dishonestly. If this involves criminal activity then it is against everything that Hinduism believes and teaches.

The Hindu holy books make clear what a person should do if they are wealthy:

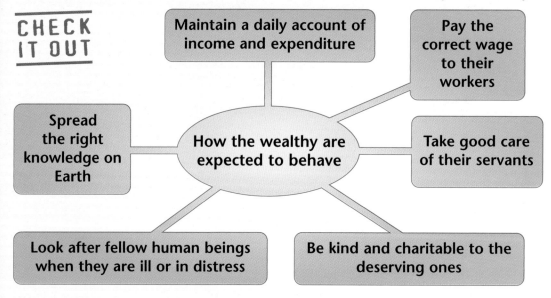

CHECK IT OUT

Maintain a daily account of income and expenditure

Pay the correct wage to their workers

Spread the right knowledge on Earth

How the wealthy are expected to behave

Take good care of their servants

Look after fellow human beings when they are ill or in distress

Be kind and charitable to the deserving ones

EARNING MONEY HONESTLY

Hinduism encourages people to earn their money honestly and lawfully. Gaining money dishonestly taints both the money and the people earning it. It is called 'black money'. It will earn them bad karma and this will affect their rebirth – a matter of great concern to every Hindu.

CHECK IT OUT

Gambling

Stealing

Being late in paying debts

Bad ways of becoming rich

Accepting bribes

Indulging in a lavish lifestyle

Paying low wages to employees

India is a country in which the two extremes of wealth and poverty can be clearly seen.

TAKE TIME TO THINK

How do you think other people might be hurt by the way that you earn your money? Give some examples of how this might happen.

OVER TO **YOU** ▶▶▶

1 How are wealthy Hindus expected to behave?
2 What do Hindus mean when they talk of 'black money'?
3 Describe some of the bad ways in which a Hindu might try to gain money.

SHOWING CHARITY TO OTHERS

You will find out

- About the work of people in the UK to help the poor in India.

- The example of the Swaminarayan Mission in the UK.

- The link between charity and the Hindu belief in reincarnation.

In the glossary

Atithi

Karma

Reincarnation

Giving to those who are less fortunate than yourself is a very important teaching in the Hindu holy books. They teach that, when charity is shown to others, it stores up good karma for the giver in the next life – so making it possible for them to be reborn at a higher level. Those who are able to spare cash, food or clothes are expected to give them to the needy in their area.

Before their midday meal, many Hindu families in India arrange to give food to at least one needy person locally. Beggars are also given cash and they are often found at railway stations, bus stations and outside temples, waiting for these gifts. This is why the sight of people begging in the street is so common in India. It is a religious duty to provide for them. There is also a Hindu custom that a spare place should be left at the Hindu table at mealtimes for the **atithi** [the unexpected guest].

CHARITY WORK

Many Hindus also support projects to provide jobs, healthcare and education for the poor of India. Wealthy people often finance the building and the running of hospitals and schools. This voluntary help and support is so important in India.

All Hindu temples in the UK collect gifts which are then used to support Hindus locally in their area or projects that are going on back in India. Many Hindus in Britain also send money back to India so that it can be used to help the poor.

A major example of this is the Swaminarayan Hindu Mission in the UK, which has a network of volunteers from this country carrying out charity work in India. The Mission often responds when parts of India are struck by natural disasters such as earthquakes or cyclones. This is a regular occurrence.

The benefactor of this hospital in India was a wealthy man. This is the only way that hospitals can be built in most places in India.

ಮಣಿಪಾಲ ಹಾಸ್ಪಿಟಲ್
MANIPAL HOSPITAL

People believe that the only way to counter poverty in India is to educate the next generation of children.

CHARITY AND REINCARNATION

As we have seen many times, Hindus blame an individual's suffering on bad karma from a previous life. The needy in society are also believed to be suffering because of bad karma in a previous existence. Here are three examples of how this might work:

- An orphan's bad karma, for instance, is held responsible for the death of his or her parents.
- The poor may have caused someone to starve in a previous life and so are thought to be being punished.
- The mentally ill and the physically disabled may have inflicted cruelty on someone in a previous life and so are believed to be receiving punishment.

This argument is put forward by many Hindus to explain why they do not do more to support and help the needy. If someone is suffering in this life and they deserve it because of something they have done, then there is little point in trying to help them. This is the way that many Hindus argue. Non-Hindus, however, believe that the law of karma is a very harsh belief, leading to a great deal of unnecessary suffering.

TAKE TIME TO THINK

How do you think someone might use the law of karma to excuse themselves from trying to help the poor and needy?

OVER TO YOU ▶▶▶

1 What is one way that a Hindu might build up good karma, according to the Hindu holy books?

2 Describe one practical way that a Hindu might try to meet the needs of those who are poor and hungry.

3 a) Do Hindus living in this country feel the need to try to help their fellow human beings back in India?

   b) How might they try to do this?

4 Give three examples of how the law of karma might work.

TWO HINDU CHARITIES

You will find out

- About ISKCON – The International Society for Krishna Consciousness.

- About Sewa International.

In the glossary

Atithi

Krishna

Prashad

Hospitality is considered to be very important in the Hindu community. There is an old Hindu custom that a place should be left at mealtimes for the atithi [the unexpected guest].

India is one of the poorest countries in the world and there are many Hindu charities seeking to meet the needs of the country's very large population. Here we will look at two of the most successful:

ISKCON

The ISKCON [International Society for Krishna Conscioness] Food For Life programme sets out very clearly the reason for its existence in extract A:

A *"To establish massive free prashad [sanctified food offered to God] distribution programmes all over the world, so that all beings are adequately nourished with Krishna prashad, and there shall be no unnecessary hunger anywhere."*

Mission statement

WHAT ISKCON DOES

- It has Hare Krishna devotees around the world who bring much-needed food relief to people suffering from wars, natural disasters, homelessness and poverty. The founder of the Food for All programme instructed devotees that no-one should be allowed to go hungry if they live within ten miles of their nearest Hare Krishna temple.

- The food that is distributed is made up of pure vegetarian ingredients [grains, dairy produce and vegetarian fruit but not including any meat, fish or eggs]. The food has been cooked with love and offered to Krishna before being distributed. In this way, the bodies of people are nourished, but prashad also brings spiritual blessings, ultimately resulting in love. It therefore brings relief from the four material miseries – birth, disease, old age and death.

- ISKCON has several distribution points in the UK, including Soho in London, Belfast, Birmingham, Newcastle and West Wales.

You can find out more about the work of ISKCON by looking at www.iskcon.com.

> ISKCON is now distributing vegetarian food in over 60 countries.

SEWA INTERNATIONAL

There is a strong motivation for helping the poor and hungry in the Hindu scriptures, as you can see from extract B:

B *"The gods have not ordained hunger to be our death: even to the well-fed death comes in various shapes. The riches of those who are generous never waste away, while those who will not give find none to comfort them."*

Rig-Veda 10.117

Sewa International is an organisation run entirely by volunteers, set up by the Hindu Swayamsevak Sangh. Its main work is to respond to natural and man-made disasters by providing help and funds.

In 2004, Sewa International launched an appeal for victims of the Bihar and Assam floods in India, which killed and injured thousands, as well as sweeping away thousands of homes and livelihoods. At the end of 2004, it made an appeal for funds to help rebuild shattered lives after the tsunami struck many countries in the Indian Ocean area. In July 2005, it appealed for help to meet the needs of those who were victims of the bomb attacks which hit London.

You can find out more about the work of Sewa International by looking at www.sewainternational.com.

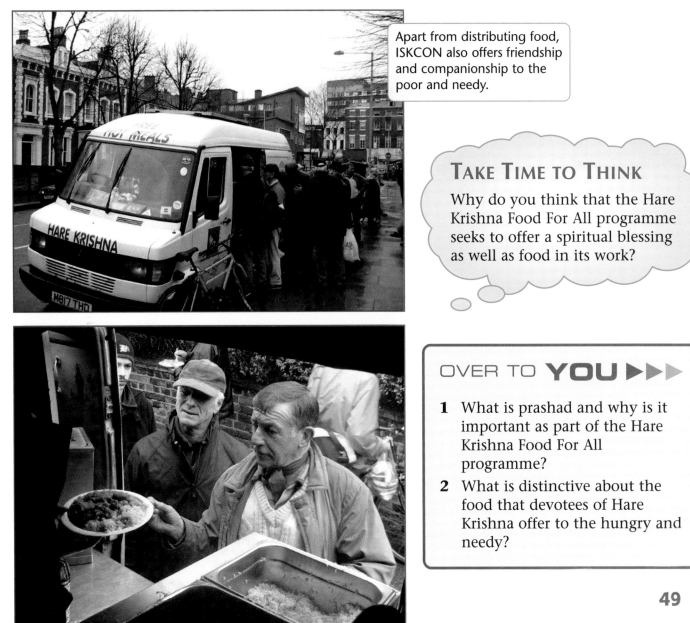

Apart from distributing food, ISKCON also offers friendship and companionship to the poor and needy.

TAKE TIME TO THINK

Why do you think that the Hare Krishna Food For All programme seeks to offer a spiritual blessing as well as food in its work?

OVER TO **YOU** ▶▶▶

1 What is prashad and why is it important as part of the Hare Krishna Food For All programme?

2 What is distinctive about the food that devotees of Hare Krishna offer to the hungry and needy?

HINDUS AND CREATION

You will find out

- The idea of the eternal creation of the universe held by Hindus.

- The Hindu belief that everything – including the whole of nature and human life – is one.

- The importance of sacrifice in the world of nature.

In the glossary

Brahma

Brahman

Evolution

Reincarnation

Rig-Veda

Brahma, the Creator-God, was responsible for recreating the world when it ceased to exist.

The Hindu approach to the creation of the universe is very different to that found in other religions. To begin with, there is not a single account of creation as there are in most holy books, since there are many holy books in Hinduism, as we saw in unit 18, and most of them carry hints about how it took place.

HINDUS AND CREATION

Hindus believe that:

- **The universe did not have a beginning in time.** Creation is eternal. This is a very different way of thinking about history. Christians, Jews and Muslims believe that history has a beginning, a middle and an end. You probably think so too.

Hindus, however, believe that history goes round in a cycle until it has reached full cycle – and then it begins again. There have been many of these cycles since time began. During this time, many different universes have also come into existence and then disintegrated.

- **All of nature and the whole of life were created by God [Brahman].** Everything is one and God is present in all nature. Human beings must live in harmony with all of nature. After many reincarnations, human beings hope to be absorbed into nature – and into God.

- **The balance of the universe is maintained by continual sacrifice.** The five elements – ether, water, air, earth and fire – continually sacrifice themselves and the same goes on in the rest of nature:

  - the world of plants gives itself up to sustain the animal and human world.
  - the world of animals continually sacrifices itself to sustain the animal and the human world.
  - human beings sacrifice themselves in different ways to look after their children and raise the next generation.

- **The universe follows a cycle of destruction and recreation.** As one universe ends, so another is ready to be recreated. There comes a time, however, when the universe is so evil that recreation is not possible.

The last age ended with a great flood which destroyed the universe but Brahma, the Creator-God, was asleep so there was a time when nothing existed. It was only when Brahma awoke from his sleep that the new universe began to take shape.

In extract A, the Rig-Veda, one of Hinduism's most important holy books, speaks of the time when Brahma was asleep and nothing in the universe existed.

A　"*Then neither Being nor Not-Being was. Nor Atmosphere, nor firmament, nor what is beyond. What did it encompass? Where? In whose protection? What was water, the deep, unfathomable?*"

Rig-Veda. X CXXIX

HINDUISM AND SCIENCE

As you can imagine, the Hindu idea of creation fits in well with the scientific theory of **evolution**. There is no real conflict between the teachings of science and those of Hinduism.

TAKE TIME TO THINK

Think about the idea of nature continually sacrificing itself to sustain other parts of the universe. Come up with five examples to show how important this is.

OVER TO **YOU** ▶▶▶

1 Write down five bullet points summarising what Hindus believe about the creation of the universe.

2 Here is something for you to chew on. Think about the idea of time going round in a cycle. Think about the Hindu belief in reincarnation. How do the two beliefs fit together.

FORESTS, TREES AND HINDUS

THE FOREST

The environment is very precious to Hindus and this is especially true of forested areas. The fourth ashrama [unit 4] is that of the forest-dweller, following the student, householder and retirement stages in life. Hindus believe that forests are pure nature, untouched by humans, and it is by living there that people can find union with God.

According to Hindu legend, the god Krishna spent much of his time in the forest and this makes it very special. Certain trees are also thought to be very special, such as the banyan tree. It was while sitting beneath this tree that the Buddha was 'enlightened'.

ARC

The Alliance of Religion and Conservation [ARC] brings together different religions which share a common concern for the environment. They work together on many projects to save or help the world in which we live.

One project shows the way in which religious and conservation interests can come together. Vrindivan is a major Hindu pilgrimage centre, but the forests of the area were being destroyed so that the city could expand. When the very last tree of any size in the area was destroyed, a campaign was launched to replant trees along the route that pilgrims took to Vrindivan.

In recent years, thousands of trees have been planted, local people have been educated about the importance of trees to conservation and children have been encouraged to learn about the importance of the work.

You can find out more about ARC from www.arcworld.org.

A *"Nature enjoys being enjoyed, but reacts furiously to exploitation. Today's situation is caused by our separation from Krishna and his message of commitment. Let us act on his message to play, not to exploit."*

Vrindivan Declaration

OVER TO **YOU** ▶▶▶

1 Visit the website of ARC to find out about three projects which the organisation is responsible for organising.
2 Find out why the health and existence of trees is absolutely essential for the future health of the environment and write some notes up in your book.
3 Visit the website of the Chipko Movement to find out about some of the projects that the movement is responsible for organising. [www.arcworld.org]

Hugging a tree to protect it.

THE CHIPKO MOVEMENT

Some 300 years ago, the followers of a Hindu sect, led by a woman, decided to protect trees from woodcutters by embracing the trees so that workmen would harm them rather than the trees.

In 1974, a group of women hugged the trees that were about to be cut down by a sports goods company, as they knew that this would ruin their lives. Some of the tree-huggers remembered a teacher in the 15th century who had taught that human beings would themselves be destroyed if they destroyed nature.

So the Chipko [Hug-a–Tree] Movement began. This movement, mainly made up of women, was determined that the rapid growth of industry that was taking place in India should not be allowed to destroy the environment. The movement continues today.

TAKE TIME TO THINK

What do you think are some of the practical ways in which human beings can protect nature?

CARING FOR THE ENVIRONMENT

WHY HINDUS CARE FOR THE ENVIRONMENT

There are many reasons why Hindus are under a strong obligation to protect and care for the environment:

- There is a strong link between many Hindu deities and animals. Some of the avatars of the god Vishnu have taken on an animal form – such as the mouse, the boar and the tortoise.

- The Hindu belief in reincarnation and karma. Harming and destroying the environment is believed by most Hindus to be a way to create bad karma.

- The Hindu belief in **ahimsa** teaches strongly that it is wrong to harm or destroy any form of life unless it is for an overwhelming reason.

Nandi, one of the many Hindu deities which take an animal form.

PUTTING CONCERN INTO PRACTICE

It has long been the teaching of both Hinduism and Judaism that nothing should be done to harm trees – especially during a battle. If a tree has to be cut down then another tree should be planted elsewhere. When a new building is erected, there is a special ceremony because some destruction of the habitat is bound to be involved – and the new building is resting on the Earth.

Many Hindus are vegetarians, although some eat meat. Those who do should offer up thanks to their god for the food that they eat as well as to ask the forgiveness of the animal they killed for the meat.

A *"I am the food of life."*

Taittiriya Upanishad 3

The problem faced by millions of Hindus is that their poverty often forces them to ignore any concern for the environment. For these people, survival is what matters most. Hindu industrialists also often ignore environmental concerns when it comes to erecting new shopping malls and houses.

ISKCON

The International Society for Krishna Consciousness [ISKCON] is one of the most successful Hindu societies. It concerns itself with 'matters of the spirit' and is dedicated worldwide to living and teaching Hindu culture. This it does through a confederation of temples, farms, communities and individuals, using chanting and yoga to nurture a love of God and a return to the spiritual world.

Putting basic Hindu principles into practice, ISKCON believes that accepting the principle of ahimsa means that its followers should live a life in harmony with the planet by following an eco-friendly and vegetarian lifestyle.

You can find out more about ISKCON by visiting www.iskcon.org.uk or www.iskcon.com.

B *"O Goddess Earth, whose garments are the oceans and ornaments, the hills and mountain ranges; please forgive me as I walk on you today."*
Hindu prayer addressed to the Earth

TAKE TIME TO THINK

Hindus believe that the different parts of nature – such as the earth, the lakes and rivers, the sun and the moon – are living, just as humans and animals are living. For this reason, human beings should apologise to them if they harm them by what they do. Do you think it would make a difference to the environment if everyone did this?

OVER TO **YOU** ▶▶▶

1 Find pictures of two Hindu deities which have taken on an animal form. Copy them into your book and write down what you can find out about each of the deities.

2 Describe three reasons why many Hindus feel that they have a responsibility to take care of the environment.

SHOWING REVERENCE FOR ANIMALS

You will find out

- The reasons why Hindus have a great reverence for life.

- The reverence that Hindus show for plants and animals.

- The importance of the cow in Hinduism.

In the glossary

Ahimsa

Ganesha

Hanuman

Reincarnation

Shiva

Vishnu

There is a well-known Hindu saying:

A *"The Earth is our mother and we are all her children."*

Respect for the Earth and for all forms of life is a very important part of Hindu teaching. There are three reasons for this:

- The idea of ahimsa [unit 28].
- The Hindu belief in reincarnation [unit 11].
- The belief that God dwells in all forms of life.

These three beliefs mean that, to a Hindu, harming an animal is just like harming a friend or a member of their family.

REVERENCE FOR PLANTS AND ANIMALS

Hindus have a great reverence for some plants because of their medicinal qualities. Sometimes they revere plants because of the links that they have with the Hindu gods or goddesses. So the tuli is sacred to the followers of Vishnu, while the followers of Shiva revere the bilva or bel tree. Followers use these plants in their worship.

Some animals are also highly revered because of their links with the Hindu gods.

CHECK IT OUT

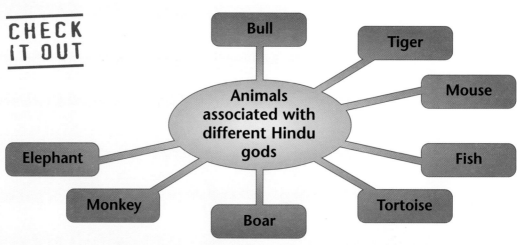

Monkeys are treated by many Hindus as sacred because of their association with Hanuman, the monkey-god. The same is also true of elephants because of the god Ganesha.

Hindu prayers recognise that, in tilling the land, many animals will be killed accidentally. Here is a prayer which Hindus use to guard against this happening:

B *"A householder has five slaughterhouses: the hearth, the millstone, the broom, the mortar and the water-jar. By using these he sins."*

It is against the law to kill a cow, even accidentally, in India.

THE SACRED COW

The most sacred of all animals to Hindus is the cow. By showing a reverence for it, Hindus are expressing their gratitude for life itself. The cow is a great source of nourishment and the giver of life itself in the villages of India. It provides:

- Milk
- Butter
- Yoghurt
- Dung for manure and plastering walls

Bullocks are also essential for drawing and pulling carts. The god Shiva is often pictured riding on a bullock and temples are often dedicated to them. It is forbidden to kill a cow in India and there are even 'retirement homes' for them.

Hanuman, the monkey-god, is among the most loved of all Hindu deities.

TAKE TIME TO THINK

Why do you think that the Hindu beliefs in reincarnation and God dwelling in all forms of life should lead to a reverence for all life?

OVER TO **YOU** ▶▶▶

1 Write a paragraph to explain what you think Hindus mean when they say: "The Earth is our mother and we are all her children."
2 How do Hindus show their belief that the cow is the holiest of all animals?

AHIMSA

These Hindu pilgrims are washing on the banks of the River Ganges. They all share a strong belief in the doctrine of ahimsa.

The Buddha, the founder of Buddhism, was just one of many Indian teachers who taught their followers the doctrine of ahimsa. Both Buddhism and Hinduism teach that no living creature should be harmed.

WHAT IS AHIMSA?

We saw in unit 19 that a respect for all forms of life – insects, animals, birds, fish and human beings – is an important feature of Hinduism. Ahimsa is the belief which expresses that all forms of life are sacred or holy. Indeed, many Hindus find it impossible to draw any real distinction between animal and human life.

Ahimsa means taking no action to harm any living thing. To put this principle into action in everyday life means that a person must refrain from any action that could lead to the taking of life – or even the shedding of blood.

AHIMSA IN PRACTICE

Ahimsa does not mean the removal or alleviation of pain or distress that is already being caused. India is a continent on which poverty and malnutrition cause suffering to millions on an immense scale every day – as any visitor to the continent knows.

Beggars and the poor live wretched lives on the streets of Calcutta and Mumbai every night, with next to nothing being done to help them. The Caste System condemns millions of people to do miserable jobs for all of their lives.

Hindus believe that this pain and suffering stems from the bad karma of a previous life and, consequently, nothing can be done about it. All that people can hope is that they will carry forward improved karma into the next life.

FROM AHIMSA TO NON-VIOLENCE

The West became particularly conscious of the Hindu belief in ahimsa in the 1930s and the 1940s. Mahatma Gandhi found that it provided him with a very powerful tool to persuade the British to leave India. He believed that all religions, particularly Christianity and Hinduism, should be tolerant and non-violent to each other. They should also teach the nations of the world to be non-violent in their dealings with each other [A].

A *"Our inward prayer should be that a Hindu should be a better Hindu, a Muslim a better Muslim and a Christian a better Christian."*

Mahatma Gandhi

Gandhi interpreted the belief in ahimsa to mean 'non-violence' and 'non-cooperation' and the British found that they had nothing in their armoury to fight against it.

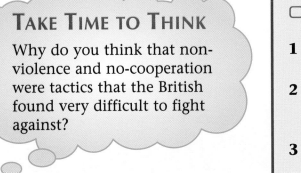

TAKE TIME TO THINK

Why do you think that non-violence and no-cooperation were tactics that the British found very difficult to fight against?

OVER TO **YOU** ▶▶▶

1 Describe, in one or two sentences, what the word 'ahimsa' means.

2 Explain how Hindus can believe that all life is holy and yet live alongside some of the worst poverty in the world.

3 How did Gandhi use the doctrine of ahimsa to force the British to leave India?

WAR AND ANGER

When the Caste System was fully in operation, there was a varna called Kshatriyas – the warriors. It was their duty to rule, preserve order and fight, if necessary. It was not a sin for these people to fight.

HOLY WAR

The Bhagavad-Gita describes a great battle in which the god Krishna encouraged Arjuna, the hero of the story, to fight against members of his own family – something that he was very reluctant to do:

A *"For there is nothing more welcome for a man of the warrior caste than a righteous war. There is a war that opens the doors of heaven. Arjuna! Happy the warriors who fight in such a war."*

Bhagavad-Gita 2.31

Hindus are not sure what to make of this story. Some believe that the 'war' in question is the 'war' against such sins as greed and addiction. Others take it to mean that it is acceptable to fight in a war as long as it can be described as 'righteous' or 'holy'.

AHIMSA

We have already looked at ahimsa [unit 28] in connection with looking after the environment and living a vegetarian lifestyle. It would seem, in addition, to rule out war because war involves killing other people – and that is clearly against the principle of ahimsa.

B *"Ahimsa is the highest dharma [duty]. Ahimsa is the greatest gift. Ahimsa is the highest self-control. Ahimsa is the highest truth. Ahimsa is the highest."*

Mahabharata 18.37-41

Many Hindus take these words in extract B and conclude that they rule out fighting in a war. They believe this because:

- They believe in karma and reincarnation. If they cause hurt in this life, they will build up bad karma and experience hurt themselves in the next life.
- They believe that emotions of anger or jealousy distract them from concentrating on God.
- They believe that everyone has a part of God within them so, if they use violence, they are hurting God.

ANGER

In real life, anger does not always get passed back to the person who started it. When we are faced with an angry person, we have several options:

- We can pass the anger back to the person who made us angry.
- We can pass the anger on and take it out on someone else.
- We can use ahimsa and stop the cycle of violence.

Only one of these choices makes the world a better place for everyone – ahimsa.

The god Krishna talking to Arjuna, assuring him that war can sometimes be justified.

OVER TO **YOU** ▶▶▶

1 What do you think a 'holy war' is?
2 There are five people in Neela's life:
   a. Sita – her mother
   b. Rama – her father
   c. Gopal – her best friend
   d. Vijay – her brother
   e. Davesh – her boss at work

Neela wakes up in a foul mood. Describe how the cycle of anger that she feels could affect each of these five people in one day.

TAKE TIME TO THINK

Can you think of any wars that could be described as 'holy' or 'righteous'? Write down one or two and try to find out a little about them.

61

HINDUISM AND WOMEN

You will find out

- The clothes that Hindu women wear.

- The importance and significance of jewellery for women.

- About the Bindi or Tilak spot.

In the glossary

Guru

Puja

Samskara

Sari

Shalwar Kameez

Tilak

If you ask people in Britain about the way that Hindu women are treated, they are likely to talk about inequality and unfairness. It is not wise, however, to judge Indian society by the same standards that you apply to life in British society. Hindu women in the past may have had to obey their husbands without question but they had real power in the family and through their children.

In modern India, many Hindu women living in towns run important businesses, go to clubs and dance, have careers as doctors, teachers or architects and one woman, Indira Gandhi, has been Prime Minister in the recent past.

A Hindu woman wearing a sari.

DRESS

The traditional dress for an Indian woman is the sari. It covers her body, legs and arms, protecting her against the burning sun, and keeps the wearer as cool as possible. A sari uses some six metres of cloth, which can sometimes be pulled over the head, leaving the stomach bare.

Women from the Punjab sometimes wear a **shalwar kameez** in preference to the sari. This is a long shirt and loose trousers. Over the years, fashions change as colours, fabrics, style and embroidery alter. Many Indian women, however, prefer to wear Western style clothes.

JEWELLERY

Hindu women frequently wear jewellery. Some of it is just worn as a fashion accessory, but it can also be very expensive. A Hindu woman might wear:

CHECK IT OUT

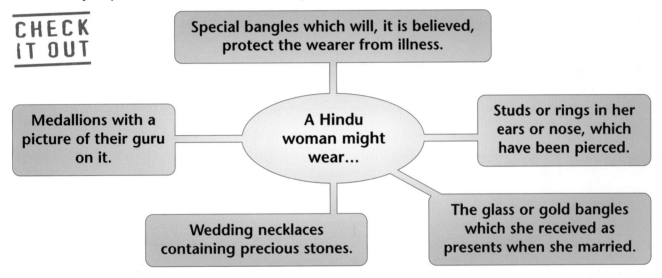

Special bangles which will, it is believed, protect the wearer from illness.

Medallions with a picture of their guru on it.

A Hindu woman might wear...

Studs or rings in her ears or nose, which have been pierced.

Wedding necklaces containing precious stones.

The glass or gold bangles which she received as presents when she married.

After having a child, a Hindu woman may also wear a gold bangle given to her by her sister-in-law during the seventh month of her pregnancy, on the occasion of the second samskara.

THE BINDI OR TILAK

Many Hindu women wear a small bindi mark on their forehead. Traditionally, this was taken to show that the woman was married but, now, many unmarried Hindu women wear it as a fashion accessory. The colour usually matches their clothes. If they have just performed puja then the tilak spot may be placed on their forehead by the priest.

TAKE TIME TO THINK

Why do you think that many Hindu women might feel that wearing special pieces of jewellery offers them some form of protection against evil spirits.

OVER TO YOU ▶▶▶

1 What is distinctive about the clothes that most Hindu women wear?

2 Give three examples of the way that Indian women use jewellery to express the importance of their faith as Hindus.

3 Find out more about Indira Gandhi and write a short biography of her life.

63

HINDUS AND SUFFERING

You will find out

- The law of karma and how it affects the everyday life of Hindus.

- The two responses of Hinduism to suffering.

- Examples of Hindus trying to alleviate the suffering of others.

In the glossary

Caste System

Extended Family

Gandhi

Karma

Reincarnation

Yoga

Suffering is an inevitable part of everyone's life. It ranges from the mental suffering of studying for exams to the suffering brought about by a natural disaster or fighting in a war.

HINDU BELIEFS ABOUT SUFFERING

Hindus believe that all suffering is brought about by the actions of people. Creation has a fault in it that brings about suffering. All human suffering is the result of sinful actions – committed in this life or a previous one! This is the law of karma:

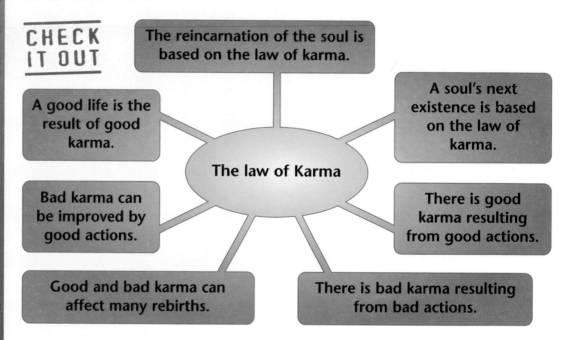

CHECK IT OUT

The reincarnation of the soul is based on the law of karma.

A good life is the result of good karma.

A soul's next existence is based on the law of karma.

The law of Karma

Bad karma can be improved by good actions.

There is good karma resulting from good actions.

Good and bad karma can affect many rebirths.

There is bad karma resulting from bad actions.

Suffering cannot be blamed on God or anyone else. Each living being is responsible for his or her own suffering.

OVER TO YOU ▶▶▶

1 Write down six bullet points about the law of karma.

2 If you were to ask a Hindu why he or she believed in reincarnation and the law of karma, what do you think they would say?

3 Give two examples of Hindus caring for those in need.

TAKE TIME TO THINK

What difference do you think it would make to your own, and other people's, lives, if you believed with Gandhi that "the only way to find God is to see him in his creation"?

Hindus believe that people suffer in this life because they have sinned in a previous existence.

RESPONDING TO SUFFERING

Two responses to suffering can be found in the Hindu community:

- Some Hindus fail to respond to suffering because they believe it to be the person's own fault.
- There is strong teaching in Hinduism which emphasises that each person must care for their own extended family [all relations] and members of their caste first. They should then care for others around them. Here are some examples:

  – Mahatma Gandhi refused to accept that outcastes were suffering through their own past actions.

  > A *"The immediate service of all human beings becomes a necessary part of the endeavour to realise God simply because the only way to find God is to see him in his creation and to be one with it."*
  >
  > Mahatma Gandhi

  – Baba Amte worked with Gandhi and shared the degradation of the sweepers and scavengers. He founded a leprosy mission in Nagpur.
  – The Ramakrishna Mission, started in 1895, teaches that yoga is the way to relieve suffering. It now runs many hospitals, schools and colleges in India.
  – The Sai Baba Movement runs many schools in India. These schools take children from all castes and educates them together. Their education is based on the Hindu values of love, tolerance, peace, non-violence and truth. The movement believes that, if children learn these values as they grow up, so they will put them into practice when they become adults – to their own great benefit and that of India.

HINDUS AND FOOD

Although there are few hard and fast rules in Hinduism about what believers can and cannot eat, a number of Hindu beliefs may affect their diet.

VEGETARIANISM

A large number of Hindus are vegetarians. This is because they believe that all life is sacred [unit 19] and so it is wrong to kill animals for food. Most Hindus also believe it is wrong to eat eggs. There are also practical reasons for not eating meat in India:

- It is very expensive.
- It cannot be kept for any length of time because of the heat.

Protein is provided in the diet of most Hindus by lentils and other pulses, together with plenty of milk and milk products.

There are many regional styles of cooking in India. For example, vegetables such as cauliflowers and potatoes cooked with spices and served with bread are likely to form the staple diet in the north while, in the south of the country, rice is served instead of bread and the vegetables are cooked differently.

THE SACRED COW

Although some Hindus do eat meat occasionally, few eat beef. Hindus hold all life to be sacred but the cow holds special respect. This fact is tied to the Hindu belief in ahimsa. Often Hindus look upon the cow as a symbol of the Earth itself, which gives freely but asks for little in return.

The free gifts which humans receive from the cow are milk and milk products – such as yoghurt, butter, ghee and cheese. These are available to most villagers as long as their cows are kept alive and in good health. This is why there are thought to be more cows in India than people!

POLLUTION AND PURITY

The caste to which they belong and the demands of ritual purity also determine a person's diet. The traditional teaching of Hinduism is that no-one should eat food that has been cooked by someone from a lower caste:

- The higher the caste of a person, the 'purer' they are thought to be.
- Food touched or prepared by someone in a lower caste is thought to be 'polluted'.
- Brahmins are at the top of the Caste System and their food may be eaten by anyone. Many of them are cooks.

In modern India, the idea of 'pollution' has largely died out. Few people who dine in a restaurant worry about the caste of the cook or those who are serving the food.

Because priests belong to the highest caste, they cannot 'pollute' food by touching it.

FASTING

As with many other religions, fasting [going without food] is an important part of worship for Hindus. Many Hindus fast on certain holidays and at other times as a religious discipline. Some devout Hindus fast for one day a week or even more often. Others have a partial fast, during which they only take liquids and certain grains.

> I believe that fasting is an important religious discipline, although I do not do it very often. It shows you that some things in life are more important than the needs of your body. Maybe I will fast more often as I get older.
>
> Sourav, 18

TAKE TIME TO THINK

Would anything persuade you to become a vegetarian?

OVER TO YOU ▶▶▶

1 Imagine that a Hindu who believes in vegetarianism and a member of another religion who does not are holding a conversation. What arguments do you think the Hindu might bring forward for the religious and physical benefits of adopting a vegetarian way of life? What arguments might the other person bring forward to suggest that food does not have any particular religious significance?

2 What reason might a Hindu from the past have given for not eating food prepared by someone from a lower caste?

RACISM AND PREJUDICE

You will find out

- The destructive feelings of superiority that some people have.

- The relationship of Hindus to the other major world religions.

- The Caste System and prejudice against the Dalits.

In the glossary

Caste System

Dalit

Gandhi

Untouchables

Hindus believe that God is in everyone. Although human beings may look different on the outside, inwardly they are all the same. For this reason, it is very wrong to discriminate against anyone or to show hatred towards them because of their religion or colour.

Dalits are still expected to do the most menial tasks in India.

DESTRUCTIVE FEELINGS OF SUPERIORITY

It cannot be denied that some groups of people feel that they are superior to others. It also cannot be denied that such feelings have led to violence and bloodshed in the past – and in some parts of the world, still do!

Hindus believe that such feelings come from within people. It is selfishness, pride and greed that lead people to show prejudice against others. It is the ideal of showing selfless service to others that is the only answer. Mahatma Gandhi campaigned for over 20 years in South Africa against the evil policy of apartheid – the policy, now dead, that treated non-whites as third-class citizens.

HINDUISM AND RELIGIOUS PEACE

Hinduism has a reputation for tolerance and welcoming other non-Hindu religious groups. Communities of Christians, Jews, Muslims and Zoroastrians have lived peacefully in India for centuries. The largest minority group in India have been the Muslims and they have coexisted with the Hindu majority peacefully for a long time. In recent days, however, there has been tension and some bloodshed spilt between the two groups.

THE CASTE SYSTEM

Many people have pointed out that the Caste System does not offer equality to all Hindus – especially the outcastes or Untouchables. Gandhi, as we have seen, highlighted their plight and campaigned for a change in their status.

It is not acceptable now to call this group 'Untouchables'. It is better to call them 'Dalits' or 'the oppressed'. It is now illegal in India to discriminate against Dalits in such matters as access to Hindu temples, public transport, education and water supplies. A certain percentage of places are reserved for Dalits in schools, colleges and jobs in the public sector. This has improved the overall position of Dalits but it has also increased public resentment towards them.

Even today, there is still some prejudice against Dalits in parts of India – especially in the village areas. The main reason for this is the continuing belief in ritual pollution. Many occupations bring people into contact with unhygienic substances such as dead animals, blood and excrement. If a person's work brought them into contact with such substances then they themselves are polluted – and they will pollute anyone they come into contact with.

In some villages, Dalits still:

- Are not allowed to use the same well as other people.
- Are not allowed to enter the temple to worship.
- Are forced to live on the edge of the village in great poverty and only doing menial tasks.

TAKE TIME TO THINK

How many examples of prejudice and discrimination can you find in the modern world? Why do you think that some people are still prejudiced today?

OVER TO YOU ▶▶▶

1 a) Find out what apartheid was.
   b) Explain why you think that Mahatma Gandhi was totally opposed to this policy of the South African government.
2 a) Who are the Dalits?
   b) How did the Dalits suffer under the Caste System?
3 How might prejudice still be shown against the Dalits in India?

GLOSSARY

Ahimsa: Hindu belief in non-violence, showing a respect for all forms of life.

Artha: Worldly or material success shown by the acquisition of wealth as one of the Hindu's aims in life.

Arti: A ceremony in which lighted ghee lamps and incense are swung on a tray in offering to the god.

Ashrama: The four stages of life – student, householder, retirement and the spiritual pilgrim.

Atithi: The sharing of hospitality with an unexpected guest.

Atman: The soul, the self or the principle of life in Hindu belief.

Avatar: The appearance of a god in human form on Earth.

Bhagavad-Gita: 'The Song of the Blessed One', the most famous and popular of the Hindu scriptures.

Bhajan: Sacred hymns or chants sung as part of Hindu worship.

Brahma: The Creator-God and the first member of the Trimurti, with Shiva and Vishnu.

Brahman: The only God who is present in the whole of nature and throughout the universe.

Brahmin: A Hindu priest responsible for the performance of rituals and the teaching of the holy scriptures.

Caste System: The Caste System is the division of Hindu society into separate classes of people.

Dalit: The self-chosen name for members of the 'Untouchables', word means 'oppressed'.

Dharma: Dharma refers to the different moral duties expected of Hindus.

Evolution: The scientific theory that everything has evolved, or developed, from lower forms of life.

Extended family: Families in which three or more generations either live together or very close to each other.

Gandhi: Hindu religious and political leader who lived between 1869 and 1948.

Ganesha: The son of Shiva, Shiva mistakenly cut Ganesha's head off and so replaced it with the head of an elephant.

Ghee: Clarified butten used in Hindu religious ceremonies, important because it is the product of the sacred cow.

Guru: A spiritual teacher.

Gyatri Mantra: The most important Hindu prayer used in most acts of worship.

Hanuman: The monkey warrior chief who faithfully served the god Rama and his consort Sita.

Harijans: Gandhi used this term to refer to the Untouchables because he believed them to be blessed by God.

Havan: The sacrificial ceremony in which ghee and grains of rice are offered into a holy fire.

Jati: Subdivisions of Hindu society into countless divisions based on occupational purity and impurity.

Jesus: The founder of the Christian religion.

Kama: Sensual pleasure or desire.

Karma: The Hindu belief that good and bad deeds in one life are carried forward into the next.

Krishna: One of the most famous and popular of the Hindu gods, an avatar or incarnation of Vishnu.

Kshatriyas: The second of the four varnas after Brahmins, the warriors whose duty it is to rule and protect the Hindu community.

Laws of Manu: One of the most important Hindu holy books, contains many laws.

Mahabharata: The longest-known poem, a Hindu holy book.

Mandir: The building in which Hindus meet for worship, also used as a community centre.

Mantra: A sacred formula or chant which can be of help in meditation, guiding the mind along a certain path.

Meditation: A form of deep thought and prayer based on a passage from the holy scriptures.

Moksha: The final liberation from the sequence of birth, death and rebirth, the final goal of every Hindu.

Muhammad: The founder of Islam.

Murti: An image of a god widely used in Hinduism.

Nuclear family: A family in which parents and children live together.

OM: Or AUM, the most sacred spoken mantra, a symbol used to represent Brahman, the sound at the heart of the universe.

Pantheism: The belief that there are many gods.

Prashad: Food that is offered first to a god and then distributed among the worshippers.

Puja: An act of worship or reverence shown towards a god.

Reincarnation: The belief that Hindus share with other religions that a person's soul is reborn many times.

Rig-Veda: The most sacred and ancient of the Hindu holy books, 'rig' means 'praise' and 'veda' means 'knowledge'.

Sacred syllable: See OM.

Sacred thread: The Hindu symbol of initiation, worn by boys from the top three castes from the left shoulder to the right hip.

Samsara: Endless and continuous rebirths in a process of coming and going from one life to another.

Samskara: The rites of passage or life-cycle rituals that mark a new stage in life.

Sannyasin: A Hindu holy man or woman.

Sari: The most common clothes for a Hindu woman to wear, made from a single piece of cloth.

Shalwar kameez: Clothes mainly worn by women in the Punjab area of India.

Shiva: One of the greatest of the Hindu gods, sometimes called 'Lord of the Dance'.

Shruti: The term used to describe the most impoortant Hindu holy books - those that have been revealed.

Shudras: The fourth, and lowest, of the four varnas, refers to the labouring class.

Smriti: Those Hindu holy books which have been remembered and so contain human recollections of God.

Tilak: Different marks placed on the forehead or elsewhere by members of the different varnas.

Untouchables: Old name for members of Dalit group.

Vaishyas: The third of the four varnas, traditionally made up of farmers and merchants.

Varna: The four classes or principal divisions of Hindu society.

Vedas: The most important, and the oldest, of the Hindu holy books.

Vishnu: One of the most important Hindu gods, concerned with the preservation of creation and righteousness.

Yoga: A series of physical and mental exercises designed to control the body and the mind.